AF725304

Macro and Microeconomics Made Easy (2nd Edition)
Study Guide and Workbook

Roggie Clark

Avoid Wasting Money On Crypto With This Book

Whether you're curious, cautious, or ready to invest, this book breaks down complex topics into plain language and cuts through the noise, buzzwords, and get-rich-quick schemes.

https://www.amazon.com/Think-Before-You-Crypto-Understanding-ebook/dp/B0F3YQ1L2Q

Learn How To Invest in Gold Bars With This Book

Whether you're new to investing or seeking to diversify your portfolio, this beginner-friendly guide will give you the knowledge and confidence to invest in gold, and other precious metals.

https://www.amazon.com/Ultimate-Investing-Buying-Guide-Beginners-ebook/dp/B0F1KWWDXG

Learn How To Invest in Silver With This Book

Whether you're approaching retirement or already enjoying it, protecting and growing your wealth is critical. The Ultimate Silver Investing & Buying Guide For Beginners is your clear, no-nonsense guide to incorporating silver into your wealth-building strategy.

https://www.amazon.com/Ultimate-Silver-Investing-Buying-Beginners-ebook

Copyright

Title: Macro and Microeconomics Made Easy (2nd Edition)
Author: Roggie Clark

Disclaimer

The views and opinions expressed in this book are those of the author and do not necessarily reflect the official policy or position of any individual, company, or organization cited or referenced in the text. The author is not affiliated with any of the individuals, companies, or organizations mentioned in the text, nor does the author receive any form of compensation for citing or referencing them.

The professional information in this text is distributed on an "as is" basis, without warranty. While every precaution has been taken in the preparation of the text, neither the author nor the publisher shall have any liability to any person or entity with respect to any loss or damage caused or alleged to be caused directly or indirectly by the instructions contained in this text or by the computer software and hardware products described in it.

The author nor the publisher does not guarantee any specific results or outcomes, and the information provided in this text should not be construed as professional advice. Readers should always consult with a qualified professional before making any significant changes to their website or business.

By reading this text, you agree that the author nor the publisher is responsible for any direct, indirect, incidental, or consequential damages that may arise from the use of the information provided. You assume full responsibility for any actions taken based on the information presented in this text.

College Or University Usage

I recommend that college deans and professors consider this book for their curriculum; as well as a resource for your students to use for their own research. If you are interested in using the book for your course or having your bookstore source it for students to purchase, you can reach out to me directly.

Please email me at **bouncerankseo@gmail.com**. In your email, please include the following information:

- Your name
- The school you represent
- The class size you are teaching
- The length of your course (e.g. 6-week course, 12-week course, etc.)
- Any other important information I should know

My administrative assistant will email you back within 24 - 48 hours with rates, and an information sheet to use for your class.

Table Of Contents

Chapter 1: Introduction

Here's to another great adventure into the world of economics. I noticed that many people enjoyed the first edition of this book, so I decided to update it with new information, fresh, new insights, and helpful images to make it easier for you, the reader, to grasp these macro and microeconomic principles.

The truth is that most economics books either rush through concepts or make them unnecessarily complicated. My goal with this book is to keep things simple, relatable, and easy to follow so you can make the most of your time.

Like I said in the first book, I am sure you might be curious about why prices rise and fall, why some markets boom while others bust. Maybe you've even started to wonder how all these theories and graphs you hear the media, businesses and politicians make connects to real-life decisions. Before you get lost in the sauce, take a step back. Economics isn't just about abstract ideas, it's the key to understanding the choices people like you and me make everyday, and the forces shaping our society as a whole.

Too many people walk around this world mindlessley and aimlessly without having the slightest clue about how the world works around them. Once you see how it all fits together, you'll have less worry, and anxiousness in your life. Learning economics should not just be about learning it to get a job, it should be about making you life easier too!

So with that said, welcome yet again to the another edition of **Macro and Micro Economics Made Easy**, in this book we will continue to uncover the power of economics and how it influences businesses, and policy decision makers. As a beginner, you should constantly be studying consumer behavior, anticipating trends, and examining new policies and how they relate to your life.

This book is designed to show you how a solid understanding of economic concepts can elevate your psyche, helping you make smarter decisions, forecast market shifts, if you are a marketer, or business owner, be able to create campaigns that align perfectly with customer needs and market realities, and if you are a college or high school student reading this might even help you ace your next exam or AP test. Because at the end of each chapter, I included practice questions to gauge your overall understanding, and at the end of the book, a practice test to bring everything together.

Also, inside this comprehensive playbook, you'll find practical ways to navigate market forces that are often overlooked but essential to winning in competitive landscapes. Think of concepts like **Price Elasticity**, which allows you to anticipate consumer reactions to price changes, or the **Consumer Price Index (CPI)**, which shows you how inflation and economic shifts are shaping consumer spending.

You'll learn how economic markers like these and others can shape your decision making. With each chapter, you'll gain meaningful insights that take you from reactive to proactive, equipping you to spot trends before they happen and adjust your strategies with confidence and ease.

In the book I provide real-world examples, scenarios, and straightforward explanations, you'll uncover how you can apply concepts like **Supply** and **Demand**, **Utility**, **Consumer Choice Theory** and **Purchasing Power** to your real life. You'll learn about things like **Tariffs** and why they shouldn't ruin your life, and **Monetary policy** and how central banks effect our everyday lives.

Overall, you'll discover why consumers like you and me make the decisions we do, and how to use that knowledge to make better decisions. This book will walk you through the economic landscapes where customers like you and me live, giving you the tools to pivot with the economy, anticipate business decisions, and ultimately get ahead. My hope is that by the time you finish reading this book you will be well equiped to discuss economics in an acedemic and strategic manner so that you can start making real changes.

If that sounds exciting to you, than let's dive in and unlock the powerful, practical side of economics that everyone needs to succeed! Okay so now that you have a solid introduction of what to expect from this book, let's start with Microeconomic principles and after that will swing on over to Macro — let's get started!

Part 1: Microeconomic Principles

Chapter 2: Understanding Supply, Demand, and Market Equilibrium

In this chapter, we'll explore the fundamental economic principles of **Supply**, **Demand**, and **Market Equilibrium**. These concepts are cornerstones of economics, shaping consumer behavior and influencing the broader economy. So they are must for college and high school students to learn. For marketers and business owners, understanding these principles is crucial for making informed decisions about pricing, product availability, and promotional strategies. Let's dive in.

Understanding the Laws of Supply and Demand

The phrase *"supply and demand"* is one of the most recognizable terms in economics. At its core:

- **Supply** refers to the quantity of a product or service that producers are willing and able to offer at different prices. According to the **law of supply**, as the price of a product rises, producers are generally willing to supply more of it, and as the price falls, they supply less.

- **Demand** represents the amount of a product or service that consumers are willing and able to buy at various price points. The **law of demand** states that as the price of a product decreases, consumers tend to buy more of it, and as the price increases, they buy less.

Although the definitions seem simple, the interaction between supply and demand can be complex. Consumer preferences, production costs, external factors (like market trends or global events), and even psychological triggers can influence supply and demand, making it a dynamic relationship.

The Supply Curve and Demand Curve

Economists use ***curves*** to visualize how supply and demand respond to price changes. These curves provide a snapshot of economic behavior in a given market. Below is an example of a **Supply** and **Demand Curve**:

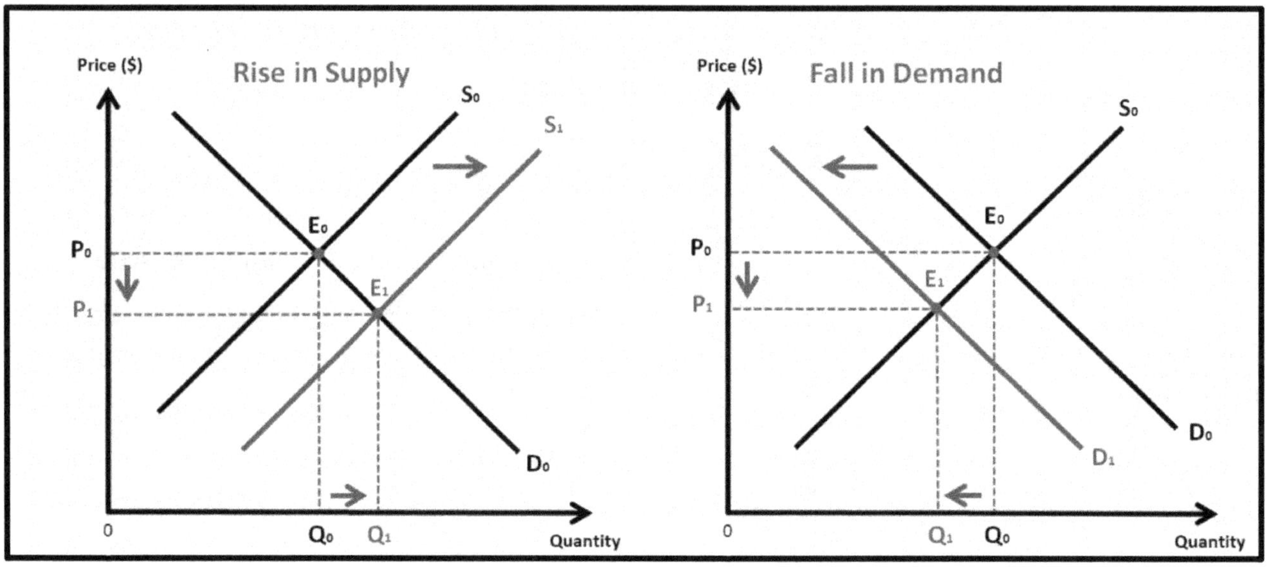

Caption: Supply and demand curves visually illustrate how a product's price relates to the quantities that producers are willing to sell and consumers are willing to buy. The supply and demand curves illustrate market equilibrium (Ansari, 2023, Figure 1).

The Supply Curve

The supply curve shows the relationship between the price of a product and the quantity suppliers are willing to produce. The supply curve slopes upward, reflecting a direct relationship: higher prices encourage producers to supply more

Typically, as the price of a product increases, suppliers are more incentivized to produce and sell it. For example, if smartphones fetch a higher price, manufacturers may allocate more resources to produce them, increasing supply. This upward-sloping curve reflects that trend.

The Demand Curve

The demand curve illustrates the relationship between price and the quantity consumers are willing to buy. In contrast, the demand curve slopes downward, showing an inverse relationship: lower prices motivate consumers to buy more.

Generally, as prices decrease, demand increases. For instance, if a coffee chain reduces its prices, more customers are likely to purchase coffee. Conversely, when prices rise, demand tends to decline. This behavior is captured in the downward-sloping demand curve.

It's important to note that these curves are influenced by factors beyond price, such as consumer income, preferences, and the availability of substitutes.

Market Equilibrium and Price Setting

Market Equilibrium occurs when the quantity of a product that consumers want to buy (demand) matches the quantity that producers are willing to sell (supply) at a specific price. This equilibrium price ensures that the market is "balanced," meaning there are no shortages or surpluses of the product.

Below, is example of a graph showing Market Equilibrium in action:

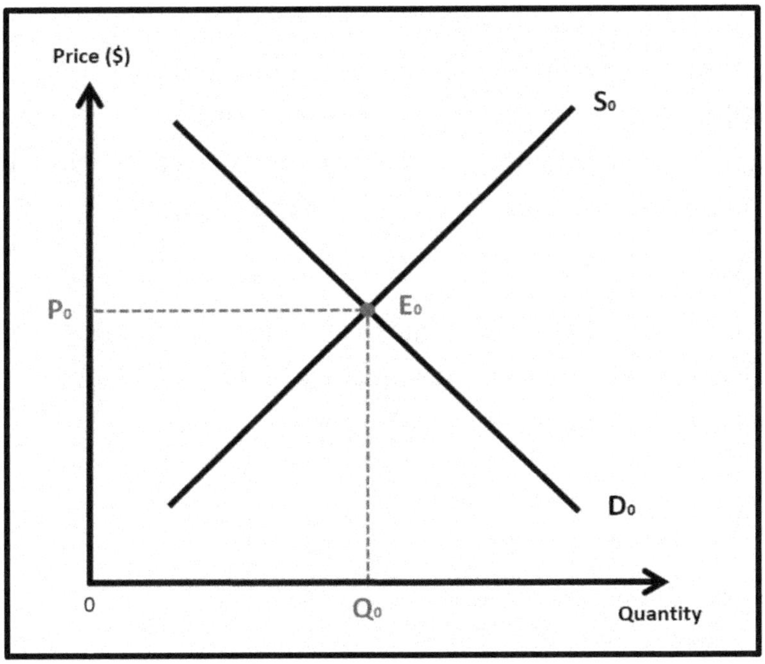

Graph that illustrates market equilibrium (Ansari, 2023, Figure 2).

The point where these two curves intersect is known as market equilibrium, representing the price and quantity at which supply exactly matches demand.

Here's why Market Equilibrium matters:

- **If the price is too high**, supply exceeds demand, leading to a surplus (unsold products).
- **If the price is too low**, demand exceeds supply, causing shortages (consumers can't get the product).

For marketers and business owners, setting the right price is both an art and a science. Effective pricing strategies involve finding the "sweet spot" where:

- Consumers perceive value in the product and are willing to pay.
- Businesses earn enough profit to sustain operations and invest in growth.

For example, during a holiday season, a toy company may increase supply and adjust pricing based on expected demand surges for specific products. By analyzing trends and anticipating equilibrium, they can avoid overstocking or losing sales.

Beyond the Basics: Consumer Psychology and Market Dynamics

Understanding supply and demand goes beyond economics—it taps into human psychology. Consumer behavior often defies strict logic. Emotional triggers, trends, or even fear of missing out (FOMO) can create unexpected spikes in demand. Likewise, perceived scarcity (a limited-edition product) can influence purchasing decisions, even if the price is higher than usual.

Moreover, external factors like inflation, global supply chain disruptions, or cultural shifts can significantly impact market dynamics. For example, a sudden increase in demand for sustainable products has forced companies to adapt their supply chains and pricing strategies.

Practical Applications for Marketers and Business Owners

By mastering the principles of supply, demand, and market equilibrium, business owners and marketers can:

1. **Predict Consumer Behavior:** Anticipating how consumers will react to price changes or product availability can guide marketing campaigns.
2. **Optimize Pricing Strategies:** Knowing when to adjust prices to align with consumer willingness to pay ensures profitability while maintaining demand.
3. **Balance Supply and Demand:** Avoiding surpluses or shortages minimizes waste and maximizes sales potential.

For instance, if a company knows demand for winter clothing peaks in December, they can increase production in advance while offering promotional pricing during the offseason to balance supply and demand year-round.

Wrap-Up

Understanding the interplay between supply, demand, and market equilibrium equips you with powerful tools to make informed decisions. These concepts provide a framework for balancing pricing, product availability, and consumer interest. But more importantly, they open the door to deeper insights into the psychological and emotional factors that drive consumer behavior.

When you grasp these principles and their real-world applications, you're not just navigating the market, you're shaping it.

Chapter 2 Practice Questions: Understanding Supply, Demand, and Market Equilibrium

Now is the time to test your knowledge, below are a few practice questions that you can answer to gauge your understanding of the chapter. Be sure to refer back to the chapter to refresh your memory, also the answers are at the back of the book.

1. Multiple Choice
Which of the following best describes market equilibrium?
a) The point where demand is greater than supply, creating a shortage.
b) The point where supply is greater than demand, creating a surplus.
c) The point where supply and demand curves intersect, balancing price and quantity.
d) The point where prices continually rise due to inflation.

2. True or False
The law of demand states that as the price of a product increases, consumers will generally purchase more of it.

3. Explain
In your own words, explain how understanding supply and demand can help marketers make better pricing and inventory decisions. Provide one example to support your explanation.

Chapter 3: Price Elasticity of Demand and Consumer Behavior

In this chapter, we delve deeper into economic principles, moving beyond theories and formulas to focus on the practical application of these concepts. To truly grasp economics, it's essential to consider the human factor. Economics isn't just about numbers and models—it's about understanding how human behavior drives decisions. This makes economics a powerful tool for businesses aiming to succeed in competitive markets.

One key concept that bridges economic theory and business strategy is **Price Elasticity of Demand (PED)**. Understanding PED is vital for crafting effective pricing strategies and positioning products in the market.

Price Elasticity of Demand (PED)

Price Elasticity refers to how sensitive consumers are to changes in a product's price. A product is said to have **high price elasticity** if a small increase in price leads to a significant drop in demand. This is typically seen with **discretionary goods**—non-essential items that consumers can do without or replace easily. Examples include luxury watches, designer handbags, high-end electronics, and gaming systems. If prices for these goods rise, demand often decreases as consumers either seek alternatives or forego the purchase entirely. These products are generally considered optional, meaning their perceived necessity doesn't justify higher costs.

Conversely, some products exhibit **low price elasticity**, meaning demand remains relatively stable even if prices increase. This is common for **necessities** like staple groceries, utilities, or essential medications. These goods are critical to daily life, making consumers less likely to cut back on their purchases, even when prices rise.

However, elasticity isn't always straightforward or predictable. For instance, during economic downturns, even necessities might experience shifts in demand as consumers opt for more affordable alternatives. A shopper might switch from name-brand products to store-brand equivalents to stretch their budget.

Calculating Price Elasticity of Demand

For businesses, understanding the elasticity of their products enables more informed decisions about pricing, promotions, and product development. By crafting strategies that align with consumer behavior, businesses can maximize both demand and profitability. This why it is worth calcuating, here's how to do it:

Step 1: Use the PED Formula

$$\text{PED} = \frac{\%\ Change\ in\ Quantity\ Demanded}{\%\ Change\ in\ Price}$$

Step 2: Determine Percentage Changes

- **% Change in Quantity Demanded:**

$$\%\Delta Q = \frac{Q2 - Q1}{Q1} \text{ X } 100$$

- **% Change in Price:**

$$\%\Delta P = \frac{P2 - P1}{P1} \text{ X } 100$$

Step 3: Divide % Change in Quantity by % Change in Price

- **PED > 1**
- PED < 1
- PED = 1

Step 4: Apply the Results

- If demand is **elastic**, price reductions may increase revenue.
- If demand is **inelastic**, price increases may increase revenue.
- This guides **pricing, promotions, and marketing campaigns**.

Calculating price elasticity of demand helps businesses and students understand **how strongly consumers react to price changes**. By comparing the percentage change in quantity demanded with the percentage change in price, the formula shows whether raising prices will likely boost revenue or drive customers away. In short, PED turns pricing decisions from guesswork into strategy.

Cross-Elasticity of Demand

Another crucial concept is **Cross-Elasticity of Demand**, measures how the demand for one product changes when the price of a **different product** changes. It shows the relationship between two goods.

This relationship is particularly evident in **substitute goods** and **complementary goods**.

1. **Substitute Goods**
   Substitute goods are products that consumers can switch between based on price. For example, if the price of a popular soda brand increases, consumers might opt for a store-brand soda with similar characteristics at a lower cost. This is an example of **positive cross-elasticity**, where demand for one product rises as the price of a substitute increases.

2. **Complementary Goods**
   Complementary goods are products that are often purchased together, such as peanut butter and jelly. If the price of peanut butter drops, demand for jelly might increase because consumers are more likely to pair these items. This reflects **negative cross-elasticity**, where a price decrease in one product leads to increased demand for a related product.

While these examples seem intuitive, real-world dynamics often complicate the theoretical framework. For instance, the shift from gasoline-powered cars to electric vehicles isn't as straightforward as theory might suggest. If the cost of owning a gasoline car rises significantly, demand for electric vehicles should, in theory, increase. However, factors like the high upfront cost of electric cars, limited charging infrastructure, and concerns about battery safety can deter consumers. This illustrates how emotional and practical considerations often override purely economic calculations.

Similarly, businesses can influence cross-elasticity by shaping consumer perceptions. For example, even if store-brand soda is cheaper, consumers may stick with the name-brand option if they perceive it as superior in taste or quality. Likewise, with complementary goods, a price drop in peanut butter might not automatically lead to increased jelly sales; consumers might stockpile peanut butter instead or redirect their savings elsewhere.

Calculating Cross-Elasticity of Demand

Calculating Cross-elasticity of demand is important because it shows the **relationship between products in the marketplace**. Businesses use it to identify whether goods are substitutes or complements, helping them set prices, plan promotions, and anticipate competitor moves. For example, knowing how a rival's price cut might affect your sales can prevent losses and reveal opportunities. In essence, XED helps firms understand **competitive dynamics and consumer choices** beyond their own product alone. Let's go over the formula that is used to calculate it

Step 1: Recall the Formula

$$\text{XED} = \frac{\%\Delta QA}{\%\Delta PB}$$

- QA = Quantity demanded of Good A
- PB = Price of Good B

Step 2: Calculate the % Change in Quantity Demanded of Good A

$$\%\Delta\text{QA} = \frac{QA2 - QA1}{QA1} \times 100$$

Where:

- QA1 = Initial quantity of Good A
- QA2 = New quantity of Good A

Step 3: Calculate the % Change in Price of Good B

$$\%\Delta\text{PB} = \frac{PB2 - PB1}{PB1} \times 100$$

Where:

- PB1 = Initial price of Good B
- PB2 = New price of Good B

Step 4: Divide to Find XED

$$\textbf{XED} = \frac{\%\Delta QA}{\%\Delta PB}$$

Step 5: Interpret the Result

- **XED > 0 (Positive):** Goods are **substitutes** (e.g., Pepsi & Coke).
- **XED < 0 (Negative):** Goods are **complements** (e.g., Coffee & Sugar).
- XED Goods are **unrelated**.

The formula compares the percentage change in quantity demanded of Good A with the percentage change in price of Good B. A positive result signals substitutes, a negative result signals complements, and a value near zero suggests little to no relationship.

Inelastic Demand and Cost-Benefit Analysis

Some products and services appear to have **Inelastic Demand**, meaning consumers continue to purchase them despite price increases. Gasoline is a common example. Many consumers rely on gasoline for essential travel, leaving them with few immediate alternatives. However, even gasoline is not perfectly inelastic. Over time, sustained price hikes can prompt changes in behavior, such as reduced driving, increased carpooling, or a shift toward public transportation.

Here, the concept of **Cost-Benefit Analysis** plays a crucial role. Consumers weigh the importance of their destination or activity against the cost of reaching it. If the benefit of traveling outweighs the cost of gasoline, they'll continue to pay the higher price. However, if prices cross a critical threshold, consumers may adjust their habits.

This underscores an important point: even products that seem inelastic have limits. By analyzing these limits, businesses can anticipate consumer responses to price changes and develop strategies to mitigate demand fluctuations.

Another strong example of inelastic demand is found in essential medications. Even if the price of a life-saving drug rises significantly, patients who depend on it, may continue to purchase the same amount. Because health and survival generally take priority over cost, the change in price has little effect on quantity demanded, making this a good case of highly inelastic demand.

Practical Applications for Businesses and Marketers

The concepts of elasticity and cross-elasticity aren't just academic—they're tools for actionable business strategies. Here's how understanding these principles can benefit your business:

- **Pricing Strategies**: Use elasticity data to determine optimal pricing. For elastic goods, competitive pricing can maintain demand, while for inelastic goods, modest price increases can boost revenue without significantly affecting sales.
- **Promotional Campaigns**: Align discounts and offers with consumer sensitivity to price changes. For complementary goods, bundling promotions can drive sales for both products.
- **Product Development**: Create products with features that enhance perceived value, reducing their price elasticity. This can help justify premium pricing even in competitive markets.

Wrap-Up

Understanding elasticity is a powerful way to bridge economic theory and business strategy. By recognizing how price changes influence consumer behavior, businesses can make smarter decisions about pricing, promotions, and product positioning. Whether you're navigating market challenges or planning a new campaign, a clear grasp of elasticity enables you to align your strategies with consumer needs, ensuring long-term success and profitability.

Chapter 3 Practice Questions: Price Elasticity of Demand and Consumer Behavior

Now is the time to test your knowledge, below are a few practice questions that you can answer to gauge your understanding of the chapter. Be sure to refer back to the chapter to refresh your memory, also the answers are at the back of the book.

1. Multiple Choice

Which of the following statements best describes a product with high price elasticity of demand?

a) A small price increase causes only a slight decrease in demand.
b) A small price increase causes a significant drop in demand.
c) Consumers continue to buy the same amount regardless of price changes.
d) The product's demand is completely unaffected by economic conditions.

2. True or False

Cross-elasticity of demand measures how the demand for one good changes when the price of another good changes.

3. Explain

Explain how a business might use knowledge of price elasticity and cross-elasticity to make better pricing and promotional decisions. Provide one example to support your answer.

Chapter 4: Utility and Consumer Choice Theory

In this chapter, we will explore **Consumer Choice Theory** and the concept of **Utility** and how understanding these can help you better grasp the decision-making process that consumers use when choosing which products and services to purchase. Let's start with **Utility**.

Utility

Utility is a measure of the satisfaction or pleasure that a person derives from consuming or using a product or service. In essence, it reflects the value that makes someone think, "This is worth buying," or, "This product or service can solve my problems or fulfill my needs."

Essentially, Utility is the economist's way of describing the satisfaction, pleasure, or benefit a consumer derives from consuming a good or service. It's subjective, meaning what provides utility to one person may not to another.

Utility isn't a fixed value—it changes based on context, preferences, and how much of the product the person has already consumed. To make better decisions, consumers and businesses must evaluate different aspects of utility.

Two main approaches to utility in terms of Microeconomics:

1. **Cardinal Utility** (older approach)

    - Assumes utility can be measured numerically (e.g., eating a burger gives you 20 "utils"). "20 utils" is just a **conceptual placeholder** economists once used in *cardinal utility theory* to compare satisfaction numerically. Think of it like a made-up scale to **quantify happiness** from consuming something.

    - Rarely used today but useful for teaching.

2. **Ordinal Utility** (modern approach)

    - Focuses on ranking preferences instead of measuring exact numbers. Modern microeconomics usually uses **ordinal utility**, where instead of saying *pizza = 20* *utils*, we just say *"the consumer prefers pizza to a burger."* Over time, economists realized "utils" and calculating perceived happiness was too abstract and not realistic, because you can't actually assign a precise number to happiness. That's why Ordinal Utility is used more often.

  - Example: A consumer prefers coffee to tea, and tea to soda, but we don't assign exact numbers.

Total Utility and Marginal Utility

While cardinal and ordinal utility help us understand *how satisfaction can be measured or ranked*, total and marginal utility take this a step further by showing *how satisfaction changes as we consume more of a good*, which is crucial for predicting consumer choices

Whether we measure satisfaction numerically or simply rank preferences, we still want to understand how **consumers respond to consuming more of a good**. This is where the concepts of **total and marginal utility** become essential.

Total Utility (TU)

Total utility is the cumulative satisfaction or happiness derived from consuming a certain quantity of a product or service.

Example: If eating three ice cream cones makes you happy, the total enjoyment you get from all three cones is your total utility. Similarly, a child playing with five toy cars may find joy in all five combined, which represents their total utility.

Marginal Utility (MU)

Marginal utility is the additional satisfaction gained from consuming one more unit of a product or service.

Example: Eating one slice of pizza may make you happy, but eating a second slice increases your happiness further. This increase is the marginal utility of the second slice.

The Law of Diminishing Marginal Utility

The **law of diminishing marginal utility** states that as a person consumes more units of a product or service, the additional satisfaction (marginal utility) from each extra unit tends to decrease.

Examples:

1. You eat the first slice of pizza—it's delicious! The second slice is also enjoyable but not as exciting. By the third slice, you may start feeling full, and by the fourth, you could feel uncomfortable. This diminishing enjoyment illustrates the principle.
2. If a child already owns 10 toy cars, getting one more may not bring much additional happiness. However, the first car they receive could be incredibly exciting.

Total and Marginal Utility in Action

Think of total utility as the overall happiness a product or service provides over time, while marginal utility reflects the added value of each unit consumed.

Revisiting Alex's pizza example:

- If Alex orders an 8-slice pizza, the total enjoyment he gets from the entire pizza is the **total utility**.
- The added enjoyment he feels with each slice represents the **marginal utility**. However, if Alex eats several slices and starts feeling full, the satisfaction from each additional slice will decrease, demonstrating the **law of diminishing marginal utility**.

Understanding total and marginal utility helps businesses and marketers forecast how consumers will perceive the value of their products over time, allowing them to make informed decisions about pricing, production, and promotional strategies.

Types of Utility (Marketing and Applied Economics)

From a Marketing and Applied Economics perspective the term Utility has slightly different perspective. There are six primary types of utility that describe how products and services deliver satisfaction. Understanding these can help marketers and businesses deliver that satisfaction in real life, and not just from an proverbial classroom.

They are **Form Utility**, **Place Utility**, **Time Utility**, **Possession Utility**, **Information Utility**, and **Service Utility**. Let's explore these types of utility in more detail.

Form Utility

Form utility arises from the design, construction, or transformation of a product into something useful or desirable. A product provides form utility when its creation or design fulfills a specific need or want.

Example: A piece of raw wood may have little value to the average person, but when it's used to build a house, it becomes highly valuable. Transforming the wood into something functional adds form utility.

Place Utility

Place utility is created when a product is available where consumers need it most. Even the best product has limited value if it's not in the right location.

Example: A vending machine stocked with snacks and drinks at a busy train station offers high place utility because it provides convenient access to items travelers might need. However, the same machine in a health food store may have little place utility because the products are irrelevant to the audience there.

Time Utility

Time utility is the value derived from a product being available at the right time. Timing is critical in making a product or service more useful or desirable.

Example: Ice cream on a hot summer day has high time utility, just as a snow shovel becomes most valuable during a winter snowstorm. Similarly, a birthday card holds the greatest utility during someone's birthday, and a wedding dress is most useful for a wedding.

Possession Utility

Possession utility refers to the ability of consumers to own and use a product or service. True value is realized when a consumer can take the product home or benefit from it personally.

Example: A bicycle in a store looks exciting, but its actual value is realized when the consumer buys it and rides it. Ownership examples like houses or cars can be more complex, as actual ownership requires fulfillment of financial obligations like mortgage payments or car notes. True possession utility reflects actual ownership rather than perceived ownership.

Information Utility

Information utility is the value derived from knowing about a product or service, its benefits, or how to use it. Without this knowledge, even the best products can seem irrelevant.

Example: A package labeled "100% organic honey" highlights why the product is valuable, making it more attractive to buyers. Similarly, a health supplement is more likely to sell if its benefits are clearly communicated.

Service Utility

Service utility enhances the appeal of a product or service by providing additional options, features, or support that make it easier or more enjoyable to use.

Example: A warranty on a new appliance, free installation for furniture, or a downloadable add-on for a video game all enhance service utility. These extras make the purchase more appealing and the product more enjoyable in the long term.

How These Utilities Work Together

Utilities are not isolated—they work together to explain why products or services are valuable to consumers. Let's use a simple example:

Imagine a child, Alex, at a pizzeria.

1. The pizza offers **form utility** because it is prepared in a way that makes it enjoyable to eat.
2. It has **place utility** because it's conveniently located at the pizzeria where Alex can buy it.
3. The pizza provides **time utility** because Alex is hungry right now, making the meal urgent and desirable.
4. It has **possession utility** because Alex can purchase the pizza and take ownership of it.
5. Finally, it has **information utility** because the menu describes the pizza, helping Alex make an informed choice.

This example demonstrates how utilities interact to create a compelling consumer experience.

Consumer Choice Theory

While utility explains satisfaction with a specific offering, Consumer Choice Theory delves into how people make decisions when faced with multiple options. This theory assumes that consumers act rationally, seeking to maximize their utility within the confines of their budget. At its core, Consumer Choice Theory examines how individuals allocate their limited resources (income) to select products or services that provide the most utility – essentially, the best value for their money.

Assumptions of Consumer Choice Theory

Consumer Choice Theory operates on several key assumptions about consumer behavior:

1. **Rational Decision-Making**: Consumers aim to maximize utility and make decisions logically.

2. **Budget Constraints**: Consumers have limited income and must prioritize their choices accordingly.

3. **Price Awareness**: Consumers are aware of the prices of goods and services.

4. **Clear Preferences**: Preferences are complete (consumers can rank their choices) and transitive (if A > B and B > C, then A > C).

Budget Constraints and Consumer Choices

The budget constraint represents the combinations of goods and services a consumer can afford, given their income and the prices of those goods. Mathematically, this is expressed as:

Px

Where:

- **Px** and **Py** are the prices of goods/services x and y, respectively.
- **Qx** and **Qy** are the quantities of goods/services x and y, respectively.

Consumers typically aim to choose a combination where the total cost of goods/services aligns with or is less than their budget.

Indifference Curves and Marginal Rate of Substitution

An indifference curve is a graphical tool that illustrates combinations of two goods or services that yield the same level of utility to the consumer. Points on the curve represent situations where the consumer is indifferent between the two options.

For example, if a consumer enjoys both hot dogs and hamburgers, they might be equally satisfied with a combination of 14 hot dogs and 20 hamburgers, 10 hot dogs and 26 hamburgers, or 9 hot dogs and 41 hamburgers. Each combination provides the same utility.

The slope of an indifference curve, known as the **Marginal Rate of Substitution (MRS)**, indicates the rate at which a consumer is willing to trade one good for another while maintaining the same utility level. The MRS is where the consumer's budget constraint is tangent to the highest possible indifference curve, satisfying:

$$MRS = \frac{Px}{Py}$$

At this point, the rate at which the consumer is willing to trade one good for another matches the rate allowed by the market based on prices. This represents the optimal choice where consumers maximize utility.

Utility Maximization and Demand

Consumer Choice Theory explains the derivation of the demand curve. As the price of a good or service changes, the consumer adjusts their consumption to maximize utility. This behavior leads to shifts in the quantity demanded and provides a foundational understanding of consumer demand.

Critiques of Consumer Choice Theory

Despite its theoretical value, Consumer Choice Theory is not without limitations. Here are some of the main critiques:

1. **Assumption of Rationality**:
    - *Critique*: In reality, consumers often make decisions influenced by emotions, biases, and incomplete information. Impulse buying, brand loyalty, and peer influence can lead to choices that deviate from rational utility maximization. For example, a consumer may buy an expensive handbag not because it provides the highest utility but because it signals status or satisfies emotional desires.
2. **Over-Simplified Preferences**:
    - *Critique*: The theory assumes consistent and clear preferences, which can be unrealistic. Preferences can shift based on context, social trends, or advertising. For instance, a consumer might prefer one type of soda at a party but choose a different brand at a health-focused event.
3. **Ignorance of External Influences**:
    - *Critique*: Consumer behavior is heavily influenced by social, cultural, and environmental factors, which the theory often overlooks. For example, a

consumer might purchase an eco-friendly product not solely for personal utility but due to social pressure to appear environmentally conscious.

4. **Limited Role of Information**:
   - *Critique*: The theory presumes consumers have complete and objective information, which is often not the case. In real life, consumers may rely on recommendations or make choices based on limited information. For example, when choosing a smartphone, a consumer might base their decision on a friend's recommendation rather than a detailed comparison of specifications.
5. **Overemphasis on Utility**:
   - *Critique*: Utility is not the sole driver of consumer decisions. Psychological factors such as emotions, habits, and perceptions of fairness can influence choices. For example, a consumer may donate to charity for moral satisfaction, even if there is no tangible utility gain.
6. **Ignores Constraints Beyond Budget**:
   - *Critique*: While the budget constraint is central to Consumer Choice Theory, other limitations such as time, accessibility, and cognitive effort are often significant. For example, a consumer may buy a pricier snack near the checkout because it's convenient, even if a cheaper option is available further away.
7. **Unrealistic Mathematical Modeling**:
   - *Critique*: The mathematical models used assume preferences are smooth and continuous, which is often not the case. Real-world preferences can be discontinuous and hard to quantify. This is why combining data-driven insights with qualitative research like focus groups and interviews is essential to understanding consumer behavior.
8. **Overlooks Long-Term Decision-Making**:
   - *Critique*: The theory typically emphasizes immediate utility maximization and neglects long-term considerations. For instance, a consumer might choose to invest in a gym membership despite the upfront cost for long-term benefits like improved health.
9. **Assumption of Homogeneity**:

- *Critique*: The theory presumes uniform behavior among consumers facing similar circumstances. In reality, individual differences such as personality, upbringing, and life experiences result in varied decision-making patterns. Two consumers with the same budget may prioritize different products based on their unique values and experiences.

Wrap-Up

Utility and Consumer Choice Theory are valuable for helping you understand consumer decisions and the reasons behind them. However, it's important to remember that these are just theories and do not account for the imperfect nature of human behavior. We don't always make decisions based solely on logic; we often make them based on emotions.

People can be irrational, and decisions influenced by emotions are common. Understanding this aspect can give you a better insight into why certain goods and services are purchased. Ultimately, mastering these economic concepts can help you understand:

- Consumer behavior and preferences.
- How changes in income, prices, or product features influence purchasing decisions.
- The impact of taxes, tariffs, and subsidies on consumption patterns.

Chapter 4 Practice Questions: Utility and Consumer Choice Theory

Now is the time to test your knowledge, below are a few practice questions that you can answer to gauge your understanding of the chapter. Be sure to refer back to the chapter to refresh your memory, also the answers are at the back of the book.

1. Multiple Choice
Which of the following best describes marginal utility?
a) The total satisfaction gained from consuming all units of a good.
b) The additional satisfaction gained from consuming one more unit of a good.
c) The total cost of consuming a good.
d) The rate at which a consumer can trade one good for another.

2. True or False

The law of diminishing marginal utility states that as more units of a good are consumed, the additional satisfaction from each extra unit tends to decrease.

3. Explain

Explain how understanding utility and consumer choice theory can help businesses make better marketing and pricing decisions. Provide one example to support your answer.

Chapter 5: Production, Costs, and Firm Decisions

Understanding how firms produce goods and make decisions about costs is essential for anyone who wants to run a business effectively or market products strategically. Every decision, from how much to produce to which resources to invest in; directly affects profitability, pricing, and competitive positioning.

While many economics textbooks dive into abstract models, this chapter focuses on practical insights that business owners and marketers can use immediately.

Production: Turning Inputs into Outputs

At its core, production is about transforming **inputs**, like labor, raw materials, and machinery; into **outputs**, which are goods and services. Understanding production helps managers allocate resources efficiently and anticipate the impact of scaling operations.

Short-Run vs. Long-Run Production

Not all production decisions are made on the same timeline. Some adjustments, like hiring temporary workers or buying additional materials, can happen quickly, while others, such as expanding facilities or investing in new machinery, require a longer-term perspective.

Understanding the difference between short-run and long-run production helps businesses plan effectively and respond appropriately to changing demand and resource constraints.

- **Short-Run:** Some inputs are fixed (like machinery or factory space), while others, like labor, can be adjusted.

  Example: A bakery can hire more staff to meet holiday demand but cannot instantly expand the building or ovens.

- **Long-Run:** All inputs are variable. Firms can invest in new machinery, open additional locations, or adopt new technologies.

Example: After analyzing demand trends, a coffee chain decides to open a new store in a growing neighborhood.

The Production Function

The production function shows the relationship between inputs and outputs.

- **Marginal Product:** The additional output generated by adding one more unit of an input, holding others constant.

  Example: Hiring an extra worker might increase cookie production by 100 per day.

- **Diminishing Marginal Returns:** As you add more of one input, while keeping others fixed, the additional output eventually decreases.

  Example: Adding a third worker to a small bakery may not triple output if the ovens are already fully used.

Costs: Understanding the Price of Production

Costs measure the expense of producing goods or services. Understanding costs helps firms **price products strategically, forecast profits, and make production decisions**.

Fixed vs. Variable Costs

Before a business can make smart pricing or production decisions, it's essential to understand the different types of costs it faces. Some costs remain constant no matter how much is produced, while others fluctuate depending on output. Distinguishing between these two types; fixed and variable costs helps managers plan, budget, and respond to changes in demand effectively.

- **Fixed Costs:** Do not change with output level (rent, insurance, machinery).

  Example: A coffee shop pays $2,000/month in rent regardless of how many lattes it sells.

- **Variable Costs:** Change with output (ingredients, hourly labor).

  Example: Buying coffee beans increases as the number of lattes sold rises.

Total, Average, and Marginal Costs

Once we understand fixed and variable costs, the next step is to see how these costs behave as production changes. Businesses not only need to know total expenses but also how the cost per unit changes and what it costs to produce one additional unit. This is where total, average, and marginal costs come into play, giving managers the insight to optimize production and maximize profitability.

- **Total Cost (TC):** Sum of fixed and variable costs.
- **Average Cost (AC):** Total cost divided by quantity produced (per-unit cost).
  - Example: If total costs are $500 for 100 units, AC = $5/unit.
- **Marginal Cost (MC):** The cost of producing one additional unit.
  - Example: Baking one extra dozen cookies costs $2 in ingredients and labor.

Economies and Diseconomies of Scale

As businesses grow, producing more can sometimes lead to lower costs per unit, but not always. Understanding how costs change with scale helps companies plan expansions and avoid inefficiencies. The concepts of **economies and diseconomies of scale** show why bigger isn't always better, and how strategic growth can either reduce costs or introduce new challenges.

- **Economies of Scale:** As production increases, average costs fall.
  - Example: Buying coffee beans in bulk reduces per-unit cost.

- **Diseconomies of Scale:** Beyond a certain point, larger operations increase per-unit costs due to inefficiencies.
    - Example: Managing 20 bakery locations might require complex logistics, increasing costs per store.

Firm Decisions: How Costs Shape Choices

Firms make decisions by comparing costs, revenues, and potential profits. These decisions often involve strategic trade-offs:

Profit Maximization

At the end of the day, every firm aims to make money. But profit isn't just about selling more—it's about producing the right amount at the right cost. Understanding how to maximize profit requires examining the relationship between revenue and production costs and knowing when producing additional units adds value versus when it doesn't.

- A firm's primary goal is usually to maximize profit, which occurs where **marginal cost (MC) = marginal revenue (MR)**.
    - Example: If selling an extra coffee costs $1 (MC) but brings in $3 in revenue (MR), the firm should produce it.

Short-Run vs. Long-Run Decisions

Not all business decisions are created equal—some are immediate and tactical, while others are strategic and long-term. By distinguishing between short-run and long-run decisions, firms can allocate resources wisely, respond to market changes, and plan for sustainable growth without overcommitting or underinvesting.

- **Short-Run Decisions:** Adjust production levels to respond to demand or price changes.
    - Example: A bakery hires temporary staff during the holiday rush.
- **Long-Run Decisions:** Invest in capacity expansion, new technology, or process improvements.
    - Example: Opening a new bakery location or upgrading ovens for efficiency.

Shutting Down vs. Operating

Sometimes the best decision for a firm isn't to produce at all. Understanding when it's more cost-effective to pause operations versus continuing production—even at a loss—can protect resources, reduce unnecessary expenses, and position a business to recover quickly when conditions improve.

- If revenue cannot cover variable costs in the short run, it may be better to temporarily shut down rather than produce at a loss.
    - Example: A lemonade stand loses money on rainy days; it may be cheaper to close temporarily than sell at a loss.

Applying Production and Cost Concepts to Marketing and Business Strategy

Understanding production and costs is not just about spreadsheets—it directly impacts **marketing, pricing, and operational strategy**:

1. **Pricing Products:** Knowing costs allows businesses to set prices that cover expenses while remaining competitive.
    - Example: A gourmet cookie shop calculates total costs to ensure each cookie price covers ingredients, labor, and rent.

2. **Promotions and Discounts:** Awareness of marginal costs can guide limited-time offers.
   - Example: Selling a slightly discounted cookie might still be profitable if MC is low.
3. **Scaling Operations:** Businesses can plan expansion strategically, knowing when economies of scale will reduce costs or when diseconomies of scale may arise.
   - Example: A small coffee shop decides whether opening a second location will improve efficiency or create management challenges.
4. **Resource Allocation:** Managers can decide where to invest labor, capital, and materials to maximize output efficiently.
   - Example: Hiring more staff on busy weekends rather than weekdays optimizes labor costs.

Wrap-Up

Production, costs, and firm decisions form the backbone of any successful business operation. By understanding **how inputs translate into outputs, how costs behave, and how firms make strategic decisions**, business owners and marketers can make informed choices that maximize profit, optimize resources, and improve competitiveness.

At its heart, this chapter reminds us that **economics isn't just about numbers—it's about decisions**. Every choice a firm makes—from hiring employees to pricing products—can be viewed through the lens of production, costs, and profit. By mastering these concepts, businesses are better equipped to anticipate challenges, seize opportunities, and deliver value to customers efficiently.

Chapter 5 Practice Questions: Production, Costs, and Firm Decisions

Now is the time to test your knowledge, below are a few practice questions that you can answer to gauge your understanding of the chapter. Be sure to refer back to the chapter to refresh your memory, also the answers are at the back of the book.

1. Multiple Choice

Which of the following best describes marginal cost (MC)?

a) The total cost of producing all units of a good

b) The cost of producing one additional unit of a good

c) The average cost per unit of production

d) The fixed costs of production

2. True or False

Economies of scale occur when increasing production leads to higher average costs per unit.

3. Explain

Explain how understanding short-run versus long-run production decisions can help a business make better operational and marketing choices. Provide an example to support your answer.

Chapter 6: Perfect Competition, Monopolies, and Market Differentiation

Markets come in many shapes and sizes, and understanding their structure is key to predicting how firms behave and how prices are determined. Some markets are fiercely competitive, with many firms selling nearly identical products, while others are dominated by a single company with significant control over price.

In between these extremes lie markets with a mix of competition and differentiation, where branding, innovation, and strategy play a critical role. This chapter explores the spectrum of market structures, from perfect competition to monopolies, and examines how firms differentiate themselves to gain a competitive edge.

Different Market Structures

Learning about different market structures is arguably one of the most important concepts to understand in economics, whether you are a marketer, business owner, college student, or anyone else, because understanding these structures will also help you better grasp the policies that governments and regulators use to affect competition in the marketplace.

Being that we are all citizens of some nation, it is always wise to be knowledgeable about these concepts. The structures we are going to look at are **perfect competition**, **monopoly**, **monopolistic competition**, **oligopoly**, **monopsony**, **oligopsony**, **duopoly**, **natural monopoly**, **monopolistic market**, and **contestable market**. Let's get started.

Perfect Competition

A market structure where many sellers and buyers trade identical products. No single player has enough influence to dictate the price, which is set purely by supply and demand.

Characteristics:

- Many small sellers and buyers.
- Products are identical or highly substitutable.
- No single seller controls the price; it's determined by supply and demand.

- Easy entry and exit from the market.

Examples:

Farmers selling wheat or corn exemplify perfect competition. If you're a wheat farmer, your product is identical to others. You can't charge more than the going rate because buyers can easily get the same wheat from someone else.

Another more intricate example of perfect competition is the **foreign exchange market for widely traded currencies** like the U.S. dollar or the euro. Thousands of buyers and sellers participate, and no single participant can control the exchange rate. Prices are determined purely by global supply and demand, and transactions are essentially identical across the market, making it a highly competitive and efficient environment.

In perfect competition, businesses, investors, suppliers whomever can't rely on branding or marketing to charge premium prices. Success comes from efficiency—producing at the lowest possible cost. For marketers, this is a rare landscape because there's no room to differentiate a product.

Monopoly

A market with one seller dominating the entire industry. This business sets the price because there are no direct competitors. Barriers to entry (like patents, high startup costs, and/or government regulations) protect the monopoly from competition.

Characteristics:

- Single seller dominates the market.
- Unique product with no close substitutes.
- High barriers to entry.

Examples:

Think of your local utility company providing electricity. You don't have alternatives because it's not practical for multiple companies to build competing power grids.

Another example would be with Pharmaceutical patents – when a company holds a patent on a life-saving drug, it is the only producer legally allowed to sell it, giving it monopoly power over that medication.

Monopolies control pricing and supply, but they must tread carefully to avoid backlash from regulators or customers. Marketing in a monopoly focuses on building goodwill and justifying pricing—think corporate responsibility campaigns or community sponsorships.

Monopolistic Competition

A market where many sellers offer similar but not identical products. Unlike a monopoly, each business differentiates its product through branding, quality, or other features. Consumers often develop preferences for specific brands, giving firms limited market power. Entry and exit in the market are relatively easy, so competition remains dynamic.

Characteristics:

- Many sellers offer similar but slightly differentiated products.
- Branding, quality, or features set products apart.
- Low barriers to entry.

Examples:

The fast-food industry all sell burgers, but their branding and unique menu items set them apart. Also, tech companies generally make the same products, but their branding and design set them apart.

Think about dropshipping clothing companies, there are numerous apparel brands that exist, they all basically use the same base materials but each has distinctive designs, logos, or reputations that attract certain customers.

In this market structure, differentiation is key. Successful businesses in this structure emphasize branding, customer experience, and unique selling points. The more distinctive your offering, the better you compete.

Oligopoly

A market dominated by a few large players who control most of the market share. These companies often influence prices and work in tandem to maintain their dominance. Because the market has limited players, firms are highly interdependent and often engage in strategic behavior, such as price matching or collusion. Barriers to entry are typically high, which helps maintain the dominance of the existing firms.

Characteristics:

- Few dominant sellers control the market.
- Products can be identical (e.g., oil) or differentiated (e.g., smartphones).
- High barriers to entry.

Examples:

The airline industry is an example. Major carriers dominate the market, with smaller airlines struggling to compete. The banking industry is another example because of regulations and the way the industry is structured; it is generally harder for smaller banks to compete.

How about the automotive industry, only a handful of companies dominate car production in many countries, and they continuously monitor each other's innovations, pricing, and marketing campaigns.

For smaller businesses, entering an oligopoly is challenging due to high barriers. Marketing strategies in an oligopoly focus on loyalty programs, partnerships, and brand trust. For big players, collaboration (and sometimes competition) with other giants shapes their strategy.

Monopsony

A market where there is only one buyer, but many sellers. This buyer wields significant power to dictate prices. Unlike a monopoly, which controls supply, a monopsony controls demand. This can affect wages, prices paid to suppliers, and market efficiency, because the single buyer can influence the quantity and cost of goods or labor.

Characteristics:

- Single buyer controls the market.
- Many sellers compete to sell to the buyer.

Examples:

The U.S. government purchasing military equipment is an example. Defense contractors rely on this single buyer for their sales.

Another great example would be in a small town where one factory or company dominates employment, the firm can influence wages and benefits because workers have few alternative employers.

If you're the seller in a monopsony, your pricing power is limited. Marketing in a monopsony focuses on meeting the unique demands of the buyer, offering superior value, and building relationships.

Oligopsony

A market where a few buyers dominate and control pricing, while many sellers compete for their business. Unlike a monopsony, where one buyer dominates, an oligopsony involves multiple buyers who are interdependent and can strategically influence suppliers. This structure often affects wages, input prices, and market efficiency.

Characteristics:

- Few buyers control the market.
- Sellers must compete for their business.

Examples:

The coffee industry is an example. Small coffee bean farmers rely on a few multinational buyers to purchase their crops. The digital advertising industry is another example, where only a few companies offer ad space and control prices.

Also, in sectors like professional sports or specialized manufacturing, a small number of large employers control the demand for workers with specific skills.

For sellers, the key is forming strong partnerships with buyers and leveraging quality or certifications (like Fair Trade) to stand out. Marketing helps emphasize these differentiators to appeal to big buyers.

Duopoly

A market dominated by two powerful sellers. Both compete intensely but also depend on each other to some extent. Because there are only two major players, each firm's decisions; about pricing, output, or product features; directly affect the other. Firms in a duopoly often engage in strategic behavior, including tacit or explicit collusion, competitive pricing, or innovation to gain a larger market share.

Characteristics:

- Only two sellers dominate the market.
- High barrier to entry.

Examples:

The soda industry is a great example, it dominated by two main companies. The phone market is another example. Their rivalry has defined the market for decades.

For gamers how about the home console market, it is dominated by two consoles who drive competition in pricing, exclusive games, and features.

In a duopoly, brand loyalty is everything. Marketing strategies focus on building emotional connections, running campaigns that highlight differences, and continuously innovating.

Natural Monopoly

A monopoly that exists due to high startup costs or unique resources, making competition impractical or impossible. Governments sometimes regulate natural monopolies to prevent price gouging and ensure fair access for consumers.

Characteristics:

- Monopoly arises due to high infrastructure costs that make competition impractical.
- High barrier to entry, that makes it impossible or extremely difficult for new market participants

Examples:

All monopolies, in some way, are government-granted.Water supply companies are an example; it's inefficient to have multiple companies laying water pipes in the same area. Also, electric providers generally have a monopoly in their region.

Another example would be Public transit systems; municipal bus or subway networks often function as natural monopolies, where one provider can serve the entire population more efficiently than multiple competing companies.

The search engine and digital advertising landscape, has seen monopolistic behavior. The United States Department of Justice (DOJ) ruled in court that one market participant was able to maintain its dominance in the search and advertising markets by using anti-competitive practices. These deals, created barriers for competitors, harmed other publishers and advertisers, and stifled innovation.

Natural monopolies often face scrutiny, so marketing focuses on transparency and community engagement. Business owners should emphasize reliability and long-term value.

Monopolistic Market

There are definitely marketplace instances where the situation doesn't explicitly exhibit a monopoly or duopoly circumstance, but there may be rules, laws or regulations that lead to the barrier of entry being so high for adequate marketplace participation that businesses may find it challenging to break in.

Thus, aggregating market share and pricing power around a few participants who have the monetary resources/capital requirements, lobbiests, political arbitration tactics, advertising budgets, established brands etc. to dominate the market and further facilitate laws to benefit them.

Characteristics:

- While one firm may be dominant, other companies may still exist and compete in the market.
- Technically there is no barrier of entry or one that is so high that new participants can't join but laws, permits, and regulations may disincentivize greater participation.
- Participants compete through monetary resources, lobbying, advertising budgets, established brands etc.

Example:

Medicaid, and more specifically the passing of the Affordable Care Act (ACA) are examples of government policies that may have had good intentions, but has lead to less options in the health insurance marketplace, and more mergers and acquisitions among providers which again has facilitated less choice for healthcare providers among consumers.

This is an example of a monopolistic market, although technically there is no barriers out right stopping other private insurers from entering the marketplace, but because the barriers of entry that are there are so high, and their are many large insurance providers who have significant market share, and thus greater pricing freedom, which creates a tougher dynamic for new comers to compete. So again not a monopoly, but definitely something to observe for how monopolistic behavior can smokescreen as genuine competition.

Contestable Market

A market where entry and exit are relatively easy, meaning any company can challenge existing players if they see an opportunity. The threat of new entrants forces existing firms to act as if the market were competitive, even if they hold a large share. Contestable markets highlight that market power depends not only on current competitors but also on the ease with which new firms can enter.

Characteristics:

- Few barriers to entry.
- Existing firms can face competition at any time.

Examples:

The ride-sharing industry is an example, the barrier to entry is rather low. Airlines are again applicable to this category, because some domestic or regional routes may be served by a few carriers, but the ability of new airlines to enter if profits rise keeps prices competitive.

In a contestable market, flexibility and innovation are key. Marketing efforts should focus on capturing customer loyalty and building a brand that withstands new entrants.

Wrap-Up

Each market structure presents unique challenges and opportunities. For marketers, understanding these structures informs your strategies—whether it's competing in a crowded space, differentiating a product, or navigating limited competition.

For business owners, this knowledge shapes pricing, product positioning, and how you approach your market. For students, by comparing these different markets, you can predict behavior, analyze pricing, and make informed decisions whether studying economics or navigating real-world business environments.

Chapter 6 Practice Questions: Perfect Competition, Monopolies, and Market Differentiation

Now is the time to test your knowledge, below are a few practice questions that you can answer to gauge your understanding of the chapter. Be sure to refer back to the chapter to refresh your memory, also the answers are at the back of the book.

1. **Multiple Choice**
   Which of the following best describes a monopoly?
   a) Many sellers offer identical products with no differentiation
   b) One seller dominates the market with no close substitutes
   c) Two firms compete for market share
   d) A few large buyers control the prices of inputs

2. **True or False**
   In perfect competition, firms can rely on branding to charge higher prices than

competitors.

3. **Explain**

   Explain how understanding different market structures can help a business make better pricing and strategic decisions. Provide an example to support your answer.

Chapter 7: Game Theory and Strategic Decision-Making

Game theory is a powerful framework for understanding strategic interactions between different players, such as competitors, firms, or consumers. It emphasizes that outcomes for any given player depend not only on their own choices but also on the choices of others. For business owners, game theory offers a valuable perspective on making optimal decisions in competitive environments marked by uncertainty and limited information.

Essentially, it helps you figure out the best choice to make, depending on what the other person might do. It's like a way of thinking ahead and planning your moves, just like in a board game or a puzzle. In real life, companies do this too, for example:

- If two dealerships are selling cars, one might think, "Should I lower my prices or keep them the same? What will the other store do?"
- If both lower their prices, customers get a deal, but the stores make less money.
- If one lowers prices and the other doesn't, the cheaper store gets more customers.

By thinking about what others might do, companies can make smarter choices. That's game theory in action.

Key Concepts in Game Theory

Understanding the core ideas of game theory, such as the Prisoner's Dilemma, Nash Equilibrium, and Payoffs, can help businesses navigate complex competitive environments.

Prisoners Dilema

The Prisoner's Dilemma is a classic example in game theory that demonstrates how **individual self-interest can lead to worse outcomes for everyone involved**. Imagine two people are faced with a choice: cooperate with each other or act in their own self-interest, without knowing what the other will do. If both cooperate, they achieve the best collective outcome. However, fear that the other might betray them often leads both to act selfishly, resulting in a suboptimal outcome for both parties.

This scenario is a useful way to understand real-world situations, from business partnerships to competitive markets, where the **tension between cooperation and competition** can dramatically affect results.

Nash Equilibrium

The Prisoner's Dilemma directly illustrates the concept of **Nash Equilibrium**, which occurs when each player's strategy is the best response to the other's strategy. Importantly, a Nash Equilibrium does **not always produce the optimal collective outcome**; it simply reflects a stable state where no player can improve their own payoff by changing strategy unilaterally.

For example, in the Prisoner's Dilemma, both players choosing to blame each other is a Nash Equilibrium. Neither can improve their individual outcome by switching to cooperation alone, even though mutual cooperation would lead to a better combined result.

In business, Nash Equilibrium helps explain why companies often stick to certain pricing strategies, advertising levels, or competitive moves, even when there might be a more beneficial outcome if all players coordinated. It's a key insight for marketers and strategists trying to anticipate competitor behavior and make informed decisions.

Payoffs

In game theory, payoffs represent the rewards or losses each player receives based on their own choices and the choices of others. They quantify the outcomes of different strategies and help players evaluate the potential benefits or risks of each decision.

Understanding payoffs also explains why businesses—or individuals—sometimes prioritize self-interest, even when cooperation could lead to better overall outcomes. By analyzing payoffs, decision-makers can anticipate the consequences of various actions, weigh risks, and plan strategies that optimize their results within a competitive environment.

Payoff Matrix

A payoff matrix is a type of prioritization matrix, which is a visual representation of the outcomes or payoffs of different choices made by individuals in a strategic scenario. It's a very simple 2×2 (or larger) grid in which you pit two or more possible strategies against each other and inspect every possible outcome.

This is what an empty payoff matrix would look like:

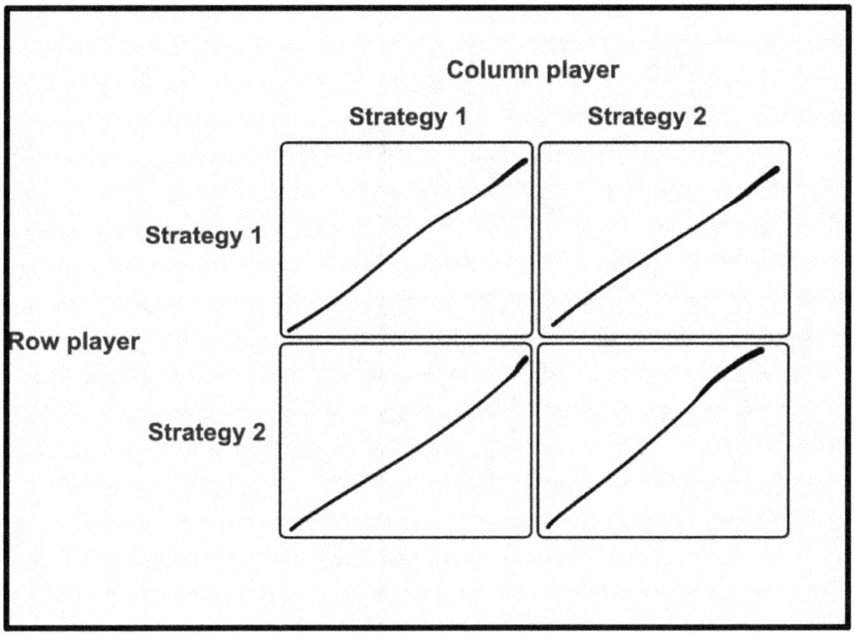

The payoff matrix illustrates potential outcomes across decisions (Fibery, 2024, Figure 3).

Let's see the matrix in action with an example in music streaming. Imagine you are part of a small streaming platform with a dedicated user base. As you plan your next major feature release, you face a choice between two options—improving audio quality with lossless tracks or adding a social chat feature. The decision is challenging because the success of each option depends not only on your choice but also on what other streaming platforms decide to offer.

For simplicity's sake, we have two strategic decisions: implement or deprioritize. The numeric value represents the number of users we project to gain/lose:

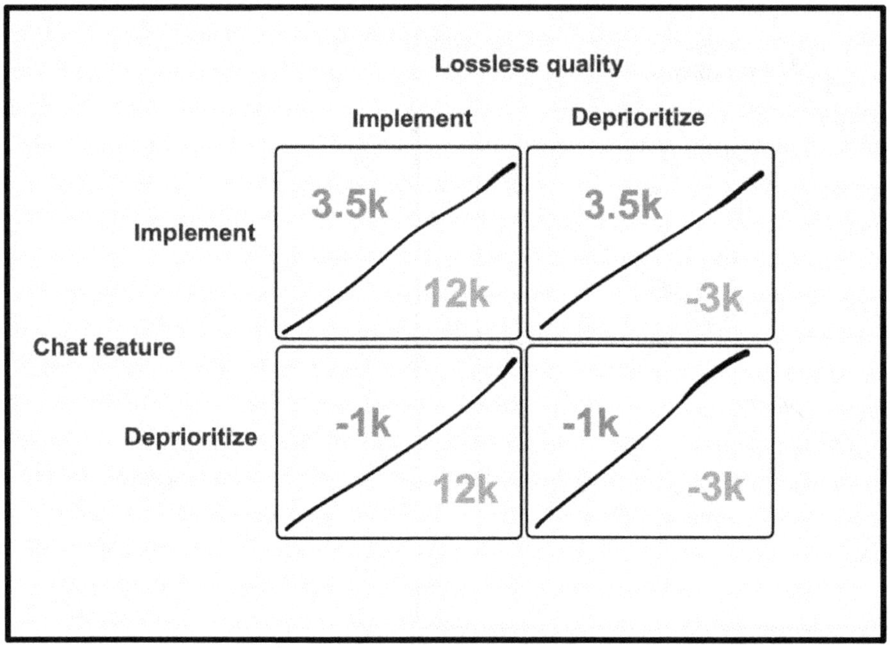

The matrix illustrates potential outcomes across decisions for choosing which to prioritize for the streaming company (Fibery, 2024, Figure 4).

It's clear that deprioritizing either feature could lead to a loss of users, and ignoring both options entirely would make little sense. Assuming that implementing both features at once isn't feasible due to capacity constraints, the first quadrant of the matrix helps us understand the potential maximum benefit if both were possible.

This leaves us with the second and third quadrants. A quick calculation shows that the payoff matrix suggests prioritizing the lossless audio feature while deprioritizing the chat feature is the strategy that maximizes potential gains.

One limitation of using a payoff matrix is that it assumes complete and accurate information. In reality, information is often incomplete or uncertain, which can affect the reliability of the estimated payoffs.

Like in our music streaming example, the potential number of new users gained—or the impact of deprioritizing a feature—might be miscalculated.

Payoff matrices also rely on clearly defined outcomes and fixed payoffs, but real-world situations are often more complex.

Game Theory in Competitive Advertising

In advertising, game theory provides insights into how businesses can optimize their strategies. Imagine two companies competing in the same market, each deciding how much to spend on advertising. If both heavily advertise, they may increase their market share but at a significant cost. If only one invests heavily, that company gains an edge at a lower relative cost. Conversely, if neither invests, both save money but risk losing potential growth.

Game theory helps predict the likely balance in such scenarios, where businesses often settle on a middle ground—spending enough to remain competitive without overspending in an advertising war. This balanced approach often occurs in industries with intense competition, where companies must navigate between maximizing visibility and minimizing unnecessary expenditures.

Pricing Strategies and Market Competition

Game theory also applies to pricing decisions, particularly in industries prone to price wars. When one company lowers prices to attract customers, competitors may follow suit, leading to reduced profit margins across the board. Anticipating such moves allows businesses to strategize whether to match price cuts, differentiate their offerings, or focus on customer value instead.

In industries dominated by a few players, like airlines or telecommunications, companies frequently base their pricing strategies on competitors' potential responses. The goal is to optimize outcomes without triggering destructive pricing battles. Game theory encourages businesses to consider the broader implications of their pricing decisions and how those choices affect their competitive positioning.

Anticipating Competitor Actions

One of the most valuable applications of game theory is the ability to anticipate competitors' responses. When planning a product launch, for instance, a business can analyze how competitors might react—whether by introducing a competing product, lowering prices, or emphasizing unique features. By predicting these responses, businesses can adjust their strategies, such as timing the launch strategically or introducing promotions that competitors will find hard to replicate.

Similarly, game theory is useful in deterring new entrants to a market. Established businesses might lower prices, increase advertising, or strengthen customer loyalty to make market entry less appealing for competitors. On the other hand, cooperation between competitors—such as aligning on industry standards or refraining from mutually destructive price wars—can also be a strategic outcome.

Wrap-Up

Game theory is a framework for understanding strategic interactions between different players (competitors, firms, consumers, etc.) where the outcome for each player depends not only on their own choices but also on the choices of others. For business owners and marketers, game theory offers insights into how businesses can make optimal decisions when facing competition, limited information, and uncertainty.

By analyzing the strategic moves of competitors, companies can decide whether to react aggressively (e.g., cutting prices, launching counter-campaigns) or innovatively (e.g., improving customer service or introducing unique features). Game theory shows that cooperation can sometimes be the optimal strategy—like when companies in a market agree not to engage in cutthroat pricing wars or agree to cooperate on a standard (think of mobile phone companies agreeing on charging ports to reduce consumer frustration).

Key Takeaways

- Game theory is crucial for anticipating and responding to competitor moves. Business owners and marketers can leverage game theory to predict competitive behavior and make more informed decisions about pricing, advertising, and product positioning.
- Competitive strategies like pricing wars and advertising campaigns can be understood as games. By using game theory models, business owners and marketers can make decisions that optimize their outcomes and avoid losing ground to competitors.

- Strategic interactions are never one-sided. The decisions of others impact a company's strategy, and using game theory, marketers can plan their next moves based on what others are likely to do.

By framing game theory within the context of business decision making—like pricing, advertising, and product launches—you are able to see how economic theory directly influences real-world decision making strategies, and how economists have used game theory to predict behaviors of consumers, businesses, and policy makers.

Chapter 7 Practice Questions: Game Theory and Strategic Decision-Making

Now is the time to test your knowledge, below are a few practice questions that you can answer to gauge your understanding of the chapter. Be sure to refer back to the chapter to refresh your memory, also the answers are at the back of the book.

1. **Multiple Choice**
   Which of the following best illustrates a Nash Equilibrium?
   a) Two companies lowering prices simultaneously, resulting in reduced profits for both, and neither can improve their outcome by changing their own strategy alone
   b) Two companies colluding to fix prices and maximize profits
   c) One company ignoring competitor moves entirely
   d) Both companies randomly changing prices each week without strategy

2. **True or False**
   In the Prisoner's Dilemma, pursuing individual self-interest always produces the best collective outcome.

3. **Explain**
   Explain how a business could use game theory to anticipate competitor actions in pricing or advertising decisions. Provide a specific example to support your answer.

Chapter 8: Behavioral Economics and Consumer Psychology

The last microeconomics topic we are going to cover is **Behavioral Economics** and **Consumer Psychology**. Understanding the psychology behind how consumers make decisions is a critical step in mastering products and services are effectively sold. Behavioral economics and Consumer Psychology merges psychology and economics, revealing that humans are not always rational beings who weigh pros and cons in a spreadsheet-like manner.

Pioneered by scholars like Daniel Kahneman and Richard Thaler, it challenges the assumption that humans always act rationally. Instead, people make decisions based on emotions, biases, and mental shortcuts—like following the crowd, avoiding losses at all costs, or overestimating their own abilities. This perspective is especially relevant in today's markets, where consumer behavior often defies neat predictions. From why people splurge on luxury goods to why they panic-sell stocks, behavioral economics helps explain the quirks of real-world decision-making.

While I hinted at this concept in **Chapter 3: Price Elasticity of Demand and Consumer Behavior**, this chapter will dive deep into the topic.

Key Concepts of Behavioral Economics

For business owners and marketers, understanding these concepts is like having a roadmap to influence consumer behavior in subtle yet powerful ways. By leveraging these principles, campaigns can feel intuitive, persuasive, and deeply impactful.

Here are the concepts that we will discuss: **Loss Aversion, Anchoring, Status Quo Bias, Endowment Effect, Hyperbolic Discounting, Choice Overload, Social Proof, Availability Heuristic, Framing Effect, Prospect Theory, Mental Accounting, Sunk Cost Fallacy, Default Bias, Reciprocity, Priming, Confirmation Bias, Time Inconsistency, Loss Framing, Herd Behavior, Overconfidence Bias, Decoy Effect.**

Loss Aversion

People experience the pain of losing something more intensely than the joy of gaining something of equal value. Streaming services that offer free trials capitalize on this principle—

once consumers experience the benefits, they often hesitate to cancel, fearing the "loss" of those perks.

Anchoring

The first piece of information a person encounters heavily influences their decision-making. For example, a car dealership might list an original price of $30,000 before offering the vehicle for $25,000. The higher initial price serves as an anchor, making the discount appear more significant.

Status Quo Bias

People tend to stick with what they know, resisting change even when better options are available. Many consumers remain loyal to their default internet provider or bank simply because switching feels too much like an effort.

Endowment Effect

Ownership increases perceived value. Sellers on platforms like eBay often overprice items because they attach more value to their possessions than buyers do.

Hyperbolic Discounting

Immediate rewards are more appealing than future benefits, even when the latter is more advantageous. People might choose to binge-watch a series today rather than work on a project due next week, prioritizing instant gratification over long-term goals.

Choice Overload

Too many options can overwhelm consumers, leading to indecision. A grocery store displaying 30 types of jam is less likely to see purchases than one offering only six varieties.

Social Proof

People look to the actions of others to guide their own, especially in uncertain situations. A crowded restaurant signals quality, attracting even more patrons compared to an empty one next door.

Availability Heuristic

Decisions are influenced by how easily examples come to mind. After hearing about a plane crash on the news, some people overestimate the risks of flying, despite it being one of the safest modes of travel.

Framing Effect

How information is presented can shape decision-making. A yogurt labeled "90% fat-free" is more appealing than one labeled "10% fat," even though both are identical.

Prospect Theory

People evaluate potential gains and losses relative to a reference point rather than in absolute terms. A $20 discount on a $100 product feels more significant than the same discount on a $1,000 item.

Mental Accounting

People mentally categorize money, affecting how they use it. For instance, a $50 gift card might feel more indulgent than $50 in cash, even though they have the same purchasing power.

Sunk Cost Fallacy

Individuals continue investing in something because of the time, money, or effort already spent, even when it's no longer beneficial. Finishing a boring movie simply because you've watched half of it is a common example.

Default Bias

Pre-set options often dictate choices. Many employees stick with their employer's default retirement savings plan instead of exploring custom options, simply because it's easier.

Reciprocity

People feel compelled to return favors. Offering free samples in stores often increases the likelihood of a purchase, as recipients feel a sense of obligation.

Priming

Subtle cues can influence behavior unconsciously. For example, playing French music in a wine shop can boost sales of French wine by subtly steering customers' choices.

Confirmation Bias

People interpret information in ways that confirm their existing beliefs. A consumer loyal to a brand may focus on positive reviews while ignoring negative feedback.

Time Inconsistency

Decisions often favor the present self over the future self. For example, indulging in fast food today while planning to start a diet tomorrow highlights this inconsistency.

Loss Framing

Highlighting what someone might lose by not acting can be more persuasive than emphasizing potential gains. A fitness ad stating, "Don't miss your chance to lose those extra pounds" is often more compelling than one that promises, "Gain the body you've always wanted."

Herd Behavior

People follow the crowd, assuming the group's decision is the correct one. Long lines outside Apple stores for product launches create buzz and encourage others to join.

Overconfidence Bias

Individuals often overestimate their abilities or judgment. Entrepreneurs, for instance, may believe their startup will succeed despite the high failure rates in their industry.

Decoy Effect

Introducing a less attractive option can make another option seem more appealing. Subscription services often use this strategy by adding a third, slightly better plan to make the mid-tier option appear as the best value.

How Behavioral Insights Shape Marketing Messages and Sales Tactics

Behavioral economics is behind many persuasive sales and marketing strategies. By understanding how consumers think, businesses can craft messages that resonate on a deeper psychological level.

Framing Effects

Example: A gym advertises memberships as "Just $1 a day" instead of "$365 per year." The smaller daily amount feels more manageable, even though it's the same price.

Why It Tends to Work: Framing costs in relatable terms reduces the perceived barrier to entry, encouraging action.

Defaults and Choice Architecture

Example: Ever notice how the "Recommended Plan" on subscription websites is pre-selected? That's choice architecture at work, nudging customers toward the most profitable option for the business.

Why It Tends to Work: Defaults exploit inertia—people often stick with pre-set choices because it's easier than making a decision.

Fear of Missing Out (FOMO)

Example: Flash sales or "Order within the next hour for same-day shipping" messages capitalize on the fear of missing out.

Why It Tends to Work: FOMO triggers loss aversion, pushing consumers toward impulsive decisions to avoid regret.

Anchoring for Discounts

Example: Displaying "Was $99, Now $49" creates the impression of a deal, even if the original price was inflated.

Why It Tends to Work: The higher anchor price makes the discount feel substantial, even if $49 was the intended price all along.

Wrap-Up

Behavioral economics bridges the gap between rational theories of decision-making and the often emotional, impulsive reality of human behavior. By understanding the principles that influence how people think, feel, and act, business owners and marketers can create strategies that resonate on a deeper psychological level. It's not about manipulating customers but about meeting them where they are—acknowledging their biases, simplifying their choices, and aligning with their natural inclinations.

When applied thoughtfully, behavioral economics creates win-win scenarios where consumers feel understood, and businesses build lasting connections. At its heart, it's a reminder that understanding the "why" behind human behavior is the key to driving meaningful and impactful results.

Chapter 8 Practice Questions: Behavioral Economics and Consumer Psychology

Now is the time to test your knowledge, below are a few practice questions that you can answer to gauge your understanding of the chapter. Be sure to refer back to the chapter to refresh your memory, also the answers are at the back of the book.

1. **Multiple Choice**
   Which of the following best illustrates the concept of loss aversion?
   a) A consumer chooses the most expensive product because it signals quality
   b) A customer hesitates to cancel a subscription after a free trial
   c) A buyer selects the default option on a website
   d) A shopper overestimates the risk of flying after seeing a plane crash in the news

2. **True or False**
   The anchoring effect occurs when the first piece of information encountered heavily influences subsequent decisions.

3. **Explain**
   Explain how understanding behavioral economics concepts, such as choice architecture or FOMO, can help businesses improve marketing strategies. Provide an example to support your answer.

Part 2: Macroeconomic Principles

Chapter 9: Economic Cycles and Marketing Response

I hope you are enjoying the book so far, as you can see having a detailed understanding of economics is not just about being able to save money, but more so about being able to plan ahead and anticipate the moves of businesses and policy makers, and thus be in a position to take advantage of any opportunities that arise.

For this next section of the book we are going to dive into Macroeconomics topics. In this next chapter, we are going to discuss economic cycles and how they affect business owners and consumer behavior alike.

Different Economic Cycles

Economic cycles, or business cycles, describe the recurring patterns of growth and decline in an economy over time. These cycles consist of four stages: **expansion**, **peak**, **contraction,** and **trough**.

Expansion Phase

During the **Expansion phase**, the economy experiences growth, often measured by an increase in GDP, or Gross Domestic Product, which is the total value of all goods and services produced in a country. **Consumer confidence**, which reflects how optimistic people feel about the economy, rises, leading to increased spending and investment. Businesses expand, hire more workers, and increase production.

Unemployment, the percentage of people actively seeking but unable to find work, is typically very low in this phase. For example, after the 2008 financial crisis, global economies entered a period of recovery and expansion as they rebuilt from the downturn.

A more extensive example would be the post–World War II boom (1945–1960s) Returning soldiers, government investment in infrastructure, and rising consumer demand fueled one of the longest growth periods in U.S. history. Suburbs expanded, car ownership skyrocketed, and industries flourished. Similarly, in the 2010s, after the Great Recession, the U.S. experienced a record-long expansion marked by steady job creation, rising stock markets, and growth in technology-driven sectors such as cloud computing and e-commerce.

Peak Phase

The **Peak** represents the height of economic activity when the economy is operating at or near full capacity. Growth begins to slow, and **Inflation**—the general rise in prices of goods and services—often accelerates due to strong demand. Wages, or earnings, typically rise during this phase as businesses compete for labor. However, this period may also see speculative investments and overconfidence.

The **dot-com bubble** of the late 1990s is an example. During this time, many internet-based companies, despite having weak or nonexistent business models, attracted enormous investments. When it became clear these businesses couldn't sustain profits, the bubble burst in 2000, leading to a sharp decline in stock prices, business closures, and an economic downturn. This where the Contraction phase comes.

Another example can be found in the U.S. housing market of the mid-2000s. By 2006, home prices had reached their zenith, fueled by easy credit and speculative buying. This overconfidence signaled the peak right before the 2008 crash.

Lastly, on a more recent note, investors and economists are now saying as of 2025, that AI (artificial intelligence) is the next market bubble waiting to pop.

Contraction Phase

Following the peak is the **Contraction phase**, also known as a **Recession**. A recession is a significant decline in economic activity lasting for at least several months, characterized by falling GDP, reduced consumer spending, and rising unemployment. The **2008 financial crisis**, for instance, was caused primarily by the collapse of the U.S. housing market. During the early 2000s, banks issued risky mortgages to borrowers with poor credit histories.

These mortgages were bundled into financial instruments called mortgage-backed securities, and synthetic collateralized debt obligations, which are extremely complex financial products that are difficult to value. Both of these products were sold to investors as a way for banking institutions to make money without having to keep a large amount of capital or liquidity on hand.

Unfortunately, when many homeowners defaulted on their loans, these securities plummeted in value, triggering a crisis in the financial sector. The resulting credit crunch made borrowing difficult, leading to reduced consumer spending, business closures, and widespread job losses worldwide.

In extreme cases, an economy may experience a **Depression**, which is a far more severe and prolonged contraction. The **Great Depression** of the 1930s is the most well-known example. It was triggered by a combination of factors, including a stock market crash in 1929, which wiped out massive amounts of wealth and shattered consumer and business confidence.

Additionally, widespread bank failures caused by poor lending practices led to the loss of savings for many Americans, further reducing spending. The resulting economic collapse led to a 25% unemployment rate in the United States and a global downturn that lasted nearly a decade.

Another example would be the COVID-19 pandemic in 2020 which triggered one of the fastest and most synchronized global contractions in modern history. Lockdowns, travel bans, and supply chain disruptions sent GDP plummeting worldwide. In the U.S., unemployment spiked to nearly 15% in April 2020, the highest since the Great Depression. Although governments responded with massive stimulus packages, the shock highlighted how quickly an unexpected event could send economies into contraction.

Stagflation

Occasionally, during or after a contraction, economies experience **Stagflation**, an unusual scenario where high inflation coincides with high unemployment and stagnant growth.

Stagflation is challenging to address because measures to reduce inflation, such as raising interest rates, can worsen unemployment, while policies to reduce unemployment, such as increased government spending, can fuel inflation. A notable example occurred during the 1970s oil crisis, when surging oil prices caused production costs to rise, slowing economic growth while inflation remained high.

Trough

The lowest point in the cycle is the **Trough**, where economic activity bottoms out. During this phase, consumer and business confidence is at its weakest, and unemployment remains high. However, the trough is also the starting point for recovery, as businesses and consumers slowly regain confidence, setting the stage for another expansion.

An example would be the U.S. economy in 1933, which marked the trough of the Great Depression. Franklin D. Roosevelt's New Deal policies, combined with gradual improvements in business confidence, helped the U.S. begin its slow climb back toward recovery.

Kondratiev Waves

Economic cycles can vary greatly in length and intensity. Some cycles last only a few months, while others, like the Great Depression, persist for years. Longer cycles, such as **Kondratiev waves**, which span 50–60 years, are often driven by major technological innovations or structural economic shifts. The Industrial Revolution from (1780s–1840s) is a prime example of a Kondratiev Wave that fueled the long-term cycle of economic growth during the 19th century.

A more modern example would be, the digital revolution beginning in the late 20th century has been seen as a Kondratiev wave of its own. Personal computers, the internet, and mobile technology have created entirely new sectors, disrupted traditional industries, and reshaped global economies in ways still unfolding today.

These cycles are shaped by factors like **Monetary policy** (how central banks manage the supply of money and interest rates), **Fiscal policy** (government decisions on spending and taxation), geopolitical events, and technological advancements. By understanding economic cycles and their causes, policymakers, businesses, and individuals can better navigate challenges and seize opportunities for growth.

Adjusting business strategies in different economic climates

Adjusting to economic cycles is crucial for business owners and marketers to ensure resilience during downturns and capitalize on opportunities during growth periods. Each phase of the economic cycle presents unique challenges and opportunities, requiring tailored strategies.

---

1. Expansion Phase

During expansion, the economy grows, consumer confidence is high, and demand for goods and services increases. Businesses thrive as revenue and profits rise.

Strategies for Business Owners:

- **Invest in Growth:** Expand operations, hire additional staff, and invest in marketing and new products. Use the increased cash flow to scale your business.
- **Build Reserves:** While growth is exciting, save a portion of profits to prepare for potential downturns.
- **Strengthen Customer Relationships:** Build loyalty through excellent service and engagement to retain customers during future slowdowns.
- **Innovate:** Invest in research and development (R&D) to stay ahead of competitors and diversify offerings.

---

2. Peak Phase

At the peak, the economy reaches its highest point, but growth slows, and inflation often increases. Overconfidence can lead to excessive spending or speculative risks.

Strategies for Business Owners:

- **Avoid Overextending:** Resist the urge to take on excessive debt or expand too aggressively.
- **Monitor Costs:** Inflation can drive up expenses, so negotiate with suppliers and streamline operations to maintain margins.
- **Diversify Revenue Streams:** Introduce complementary products or services to protect against market shifts.
- **Prepare for Contraction:** Begin planning for a slowdown by reviewing budgets, cutting unnecessary expenses, and securing financial flexibility.

---

3. Contraction Phase (Recession)

In this phase, economic activity declines, consumer spending drops, and unemployment rises. Businesses may face reduced demand and tighter cash flow.

Strategies for Business Owners:

- **Cut Non-Essential Costs:** Focus on critical operations and delay non-urgent investments.
- **Protect Cash Flow:** Maintain a healthy cash reserve to cover operating costs and avoid risky financial commitments.
- **Focus on Core Customers:** Double down on your most loyal and profitable customers, offering promotions or loyalty rewards to maintain relationships.
- **Adapt Offerings:** Offer more affordable alternatives or essential products that are in demand during tough times.
- **Collaborate:** Negotiate better terms with suppliers and landlords to reduce expenses.

---

4. Trough Phase

The trough is the lowest point of the economic cycle. Consumer and business confidence is weak, but the economy may show early signs of recovery.

Strategies for Business Owners:

- **Position for Recovery:** Use the downtime to assess your business model, refine operations, and innovate for the upcoming expansion.
- **Invest Wisely:** If your finances allow, acquire undervalued assets, invest in training, or upgrade equipment to prepare for the next growth phase.
- **Communicate Optimism:** Reassure employees and customers that your business is stable and ready to grow as conditions improve.

Special Considerations for Unusual Cycles

Stagflation (High Inflation + Low Growth):

- **Focus on Efficiency:** Reduce waste and improve productivity to offset rising costs.

- **Price Strategically:** Avoid drastic price increases but find ways to maintain profitability through bundling or value-added services.
- **Stay Flexible:** Be ready to adapt quickly as the economy stabilizes or declines further.

Depression (Severe and Prolonged Downturn):

- **Emphasize Essentials:** Focus on providing products or services that remain in demand, even during tough times.
- **Diversify Markets:** Explore new customer segments or geographical markets less affected by the downturn.
- **Leverage Community Support:** Participate in local initiatives to build goodwill and attract customers.

Wrap-Up

By understanding the characteristics of each economic cycle and proactively adjusting strategies, business owners, marketers, students and every day consumers can navigate economic fluctuations effectively. The key is balancing risk management with seizing opportunities, ensuring your decision making remains resilient and positioned for long-term success.

Chapter 9 Practice Questions: Economic Cycles and Marketing Response

Now is the time to test your knowledge, below are a few practice questions that you can answer to gauge your understanding of the chapter. Be sure to refer back to the chapter to refresh your memory, also the answers are at the back of the book.

1. **Multiple Choice**
   Which phase of the economic cycle is characterized by high consumer confidence, rising GDP, and increased business investment?
   a) Contraction
   b) Trough
   c) Expansion
   d) Peak

2. **True or False**
   Stagflation occurs when an economy experiences low inflation, low unemployment, and rapid growth.

3. **Explain**
   Explain how understanding economic cycles can help business owners adjust their marketing and operational strategies. Provide an example of a strategy a business might use during a contraction phase.

Chapter 10: Inflation, Pricing, and Cost Management

Inflation is one of those economic forces that seems to sneak up and affect everyone, from the smallest business owner to the largest corporations, and, of course, the everyday consumer. It makes goods and services cost more over time while the same amount of money buys less. But why does inflation happen, and who, or what, is behind it?

For business owners, understanding inflation is crucial. Knowing its causes, how it impacts pricing and purchasing behavior, and strategies to navigate it can help ensure your business thrives even during challenging economic periods. Let's explore these concepts step by step.

What Is Inflation and Why Does It Happen?

At its core, inflation refers to the rise in prices across an economy over time, which reduces the purchasing power of money. For example, if inflation is 5% annually, what cost $100 last year will cost $105 this year. This doesn't happen randomly, there are underlying reasons inflation occurs.

Causes of Inflation

1. **Demand-Pull Inflation**
   Demand-pull inflation happens when demand for goods and services outpaces supply. This often occurs during economic booms when consumers and businesses have more disposable income to spend, leading to increased demand. For example, if a popular product is in limited supply but everyone wants it, sellers may raise prices.

2. **Cost-Push Inflation**
   Cost-push inflation occurs when the cost of production rises, and businesses pass these higher costs onto consumers. This can happen when raw materials, labor, or transportation costs increase. For example, if the price of oil rises, shipping and manufacturing become more expensive, driving up the prices of goods.

3. **Built-In Inflation**
   This occurs when businesses and workers anticipate future inflation and act accordingly. For instance, workers demand higher wages to keep up with rising costs, and businesses then increase prices to offset these higher wages. This creates a self-reinforcing cycle.

4. **Monetary Policy and Excess Money Supply**
   Central banks, like the Federal Reserve in the U.S., play a significant role in inflation. When they increase the money supply—whether by printing more money or lowering interest rates—people and businesses have more to spend. While this stimulates the economy, it can also lead to demand-pull inflation if too much money chases too few goods.

5. **Fiscal Policy**
   The way the government spends and collects taxes, known as fiscal policy has a direct impact on inflation. Tax cuts can increase consumer spending, while large spending programs or subsidies can stimulate growth but also risk creating shortages if demand outpaces supply. Even immigration policies matter, since changes in the labor force affect both production capacity and wage pressures. In each case, when too many dollars chase too few goods, the result is upward pressure on prices.

Who's "Causing" Inflation?

It's tempting to blame a single group for inflation, but the reality is more complex. Here's a breakdown of key players:

- **Central Banks and Governments**: Governments manage fiscal policies and relegate monetary policy to central banks; both of them can directly impact inflation. For example, during economic downturns, governments often stimulate the economy by increasing spending or cutting taxes. Central banks might lower interest rates to encourage borrowing. These actions can unintentionally lead to inflation if the economy overheats.

- **Supply Chain Disruptions**: Global events, such as pandemics or conflicts, can cause supply shortages and drive up prices. When raw materials or goods become harder to obtain, businesses are forced to pay more, passing those costs to consumers.

- **Businesses and Wages**: Companies raising wages to attract and retain workers can increase production costs. While higher wages benefit employees, businesses might offset these costs by increasing prices.

- **Consumers**: Yes, even consumers contribute! When people rush to buy goods in anticipation of higher prices, they increase demand, which can exacerbate inflation.

It's a dynamic interplay of factors, and no single group is entirely to blame. Inflation reflects the collective behaviors of economies, markets, and individuals.

The Impact of Inflation on Pricing and Consumer Purchasing Power

For business owners, inflation creates a tough balancing act. Rising costs for materials, labor, and operations force you to consider price increases. Meanwhile, your customers, grappling with higher costs for food, housing, and fuel, might be less willing to spend.

When inflation rises, purchasing power declines. A family that could afford frequent dining out last year may now cook at home more often. For your business, this might mean fewer sales, smaller orders, or customers opting for cheaper alternatives.

The challenge lies in maintaining profitability while keeping customers loyal. Raising prices too much or too quickly risks driving customers away. But absorbing higher costs without adjusting prices can hurt your bottom line.

Unfortunately, many business owners have grappled with this dynamic in troublesome ways. Slang economic terms like **"sneakflation"** and **"shrinkflation"** have started to appear in popular culture to describe the declining quality of products and services.

Sneakflation refers to a subtle cost-saving tactic where companies maintain the same price while decreasing the value of a product or service. For instance, consumers have reported cases where clothing they previously bought from a brand now uses cheaper fabric. They may have also been able to return items more easily in the past, but now the return window is shorter or more difficult.

Shrinkflation, on the other hand, occurs when companies decrease the size of products without reducing the price. This has been observed particularly with soft drinks, candy brands, fast-food items, and even toilet paper.

These two phenomena are worth mentioning because they are closely related to the concept of inflation and how it can affect both consumer and business owner behavior.

Strategies for Pricing Adjustments in Inflationary Times

Inflation forces business owners to rethink their pricing strategies. Here are ways to navigate this delicate terrain without alienating customers:

Gradual and Transparent Price Increases

Customers are less likely to resist small, incremental price increases than sudden, dramatic ones. For example, instead of a bakery increasing bread prices by $2 overnight, it might raise prices by $0.50 every few months. Transparency is key: explaining that the increase reflects rising ingredient costs can foster understanding and trust.

Reinforce Value Instead of Price Alone

Rather than focusing solely on price, emphasize the value your business offers. Highlight what sets your products apart—be it quality, sustainability, or exceptional customer service. Customers are often willing to pay a little more if they feel they're getting more in return.

Flexible and Tiered Pricing

Offering a range of pricing options can help retain customers during inflationary periods. For instance, a business could introduce budget-friendly options alongside premium offerings. This allows price-sensitive customers to stay engaged with your brand while maintaining higher-margin products for others.

Practical Tips for Managing Costs in High-Inflation Periods

Inflation isn't just about pricing—it's also about how you manage costs. Here's how to stay lean and efficient:

Negotiate with Suppliers

Don't accept rising supplier costs as inevitable. Reach out to negotiate better terms, explore bulk purchasing options, or find alternative vendors. Building strong relationships with suppliers can lead to cost-saving opportunities.

Streamline Operations

Look for inefficiencies in your operations. Can you reduce waste, automate tasks, or optimize workflows? Even small changes, like consolidating deliveries or switching to energy-efficient equipment, can add up.

Reassess Non-Essential Spending

Take a hard look at discretionary expenses. Do you really need that extra software subscription or the premium office supplies? Cut back where possible to free up resources for essentials.

Focus on Retention

It's more cost-effective to keep existing customers than to acquire new ones. Offer loyalty programs, personalized deals, or exclusive promotions to strengthen relationships with your current customer base.

Wrap-Up

While inflation can feel like an uphill battle, it's also an opportunity to demonstrate your business's resilience and commitment to customers. By staying strategic, transparent, and value-driven, you can navigate inflation while preserving trust and loyalty.

Inflation may not be entirely avoidable, but how you respond can set your business apart. Plan thoughtfully, communicate openly, and focus on delivering value—your customers will remember how you handled the tough times.

Chapter 10 Practice Questions: Inflation, Pricing, and Cost Management

Now is the time to test your knowledge, below are a few practice questions that you can answer to gauge your understanding of the chapter. Be sure to refer back to the chapter to refresh your memory, also the answers are at the back of the book.

1. **Multiple Choice**
   Which of the following best describes cost-push inflation?
   a) When prices rise because demand exceeds supply
   b) When prices rise due to increased production costs
   c) When money supply decreases, reducing consumer spending
   d) When government regulations force prices higher

2. **True or False**
   Shrinkflation occurs when companies raise prices dramatically while keeping product size the same.

3. **Explain**
   Explain how a business can adjust pricing and manage costs during periods of high inflation without losing customer trust. Provide an example to support your answer.

Chapter 11: Global Economics and International Markets

Understanding global economics is like piecing together a complex puzzle with massive rewards. For business owners, expanding into international markets means navigating challenges like exchange rates, tariffs, free trade agreements, and the unique economic landscapes of different regions.

Let's unpack these concepts, explore their implications, and examine how to thrive in a global economy while considering their controversies and complexities.

The Role of Exchange Rates: How Currency Fluctuations Impact Business

Exchange rates determine the value of one currency compared to another and are pivotal for international businesses. These rates fluctuate due to factors like economic growth, interest rates, inflation, and geopolitical events. For business owners selling products or services in multiple countries, these shifts can significantly impact pricing and profitability.

Imagine you're a U.S.-based business owner selling goods in Europe. If the exchange rate changes from 1 USD = 0.9 EUR to 1 USD = 1.1 EUR, (this is just an example, not the actual rate) your products become more expensive for European buyers, potentially reducing demand unless you adjust your pricing.

On the other hand, if the exchange rate swings the other way, making your products cheaper abroad, you might see a surge in demand. However, this requires vigilance, as these changes could also squeeze your profit margins when converting sales back to your local currency. Savvy business owners keep a close eye on exchange rate trends and use tools like hedging (financial contracts to lock in favorable rates) to minimize risks and maximize stability.

Tariffs: The Hidden Costs and Controversies of International Trade

Tariffs are taxes or duties imposed on imported goods, often used to protect local industries from foreign competition. While they can benefit domestic producers by making imported goods more expensive, they also can create significant challenges for businesses reliant on global trade, and not adquetatly positioned for domestic commerce.

For instance, a business exporting goods to a country with high tariffs might find their products less competitive compared to local alternatives. To adapt, the business owner could explore local sourcing or advocate for trade agreements to mitigate the impact of tariffs

However, tariffs are deeply controversial. From one viewpoint, tariffs are seen as a way to protect local industries and jobs. By making imported goods more expensive, tariffs can encourage consumers to buy locally-produced items, giving domestic businesses an edge. For governments, this can mean safeguarding industries that are vital for national security or economic stability.

For instance, if a country relies heavily on imported steel, but imposes tariffs on foreign steel, local producers might benefit as their goods become more competitively priced. This could preserve jobs in the steel industry and bolster the domestic economy.

However, the same tariffs that protect local industries can also by increase costs for businesses and, potentially for consumers. For businesses that rely on imported materials or components, higher tariffs mean higher production costs. These costs are often passed on to consumers through increased prices, which can reduce demand and hurt the broader economy.

While these higher production costs don't necessarily affect consumers because they can choose not to purchase the product or services, or instead explore other options, higher tariffs can lead to poorly positioned businesses being unable to compete. As they become unable to lower prices and respond to more savvier consumers.

Take a business owner who manufactures electronics, like cellphones. If tariffs are placed on imported microchips, and rare earth metals, the production cost of each device rises. To stay profitable, the business might have to raise prices, potentially driving away budget-conscious customers. In this way, tariffs can ripple through the economy, affecting industries far removed from the original target of the tax. But again, a lot of economists will stress to you that higher tariffs directly affect consumers, but this is highly debatable.

At the heart of the controversy is the fact that tariffs create clear winners and losers. While some industries benefit from reduced competition, others suffer from higher costs and limited market access. For consumers, the overall impact depends on whether they gain from a stronger local economy or lose out because of higher prices for goods.

Free Trade: Not Always the Golden Solution

While free trade agreements aim to reduce barriers like tariffs and promote the unrestricted exchange of goods and services between countries, they're not always as beneficial as they seem. The North American Free Trade Agreement (NAFTA), for example, eliminated many tariffs between the U.S., Canada, and Mexico, but its effects have been hotly debated.

Supporters argue that NAFTA boosted trade and economic growth across North America. Critics, however, highlight that it led to the outsourcing of manufacturing jobs from higher-wage countries to lower-wage ones, creating economic imbalances. Small businesses in sectors like agriculture also faced increased competition, which sometimes drove local producers out of business.

The same thing can be said about U.S. President Richard Nixon's trip to China in 1972. Many economists highlight this as an integral moment in American history, as it opened the door to stronger economic and diplomatic relations with China, eventually leading to low and even zero tariffs years later. On the flip side, however, as the partnership continued, wages for American jobs began to stagnate, and increased globalization led to American companies shifting production overseas to cut costs—at the expense of American jobs.

On the other hand, many economists argue that Nixon's trip to China helped facilitate the development of a technology-based, higher-wage corporate sector—commonly referred to as "white-collar jobs." This marked a shift away from primarily production and workmanship roles, or "blue-collar" jobs. But these economists often fail to address that this shift also exacerbated an already growing racial wealth gap by requiring credentials such as certifications and degrees, which historically were more difficult for minority groups to acquire.

Both of these examples illustrate that while free trade can lower costs and expand markets, it also has downsides, for workers and for businesses unable to compete with cheaper imports and labor. For business owners, understanding these dynamics is crucial when navigating international markets, and hiring employees

---

Navigating International Markets with an Economic Perspective

Entering international markets involves more than just shipping products overseas. It requires a comprehensive understanding of the economic conditions and cultural nuances of each region.

Start by assessing a country's economic stability. Factors like inflation, unemployment, and consumer spending patterns can provide insights into potential challenges and opportunities. For instance, in a country with high inflation (the general rise in prices over time), consumer purchasing power may shrink. Adapting by offering smaller, more affordable product sizes can help maintain demand without overwhelming buyers.

Cultural differences also play a significant role. In some regions, consumers may value savings over spending, impacting how luxury or premium products perform. In others, rapid economic growth might fuel trends like conspicuous consumption, where people prioritize displaying their wealth. Aligning your product offerings and marketing strategies with these cultural and economic priorities can make or break your success in a new market.

Legal and regulatory frameworks also need consideration. Trade agreements, environmental regulations, and labor laws vary widely between countries and can significantly impact your operations. For instance, countries with strict environmental policies might require changes to packaging or production methods, while others with relaxed trade barriers might offer cost-saving opportunities.

Real-World Examples: Adapting to Economic Environments

Consider a business owner expanding into a region with high tariffs on imported goods. To remain competitive, the business might set up a local manufacturing facility. This not only avoids tariffs but also builds goodwill by supporting the local economy through job creation.

In another case, a business entering a country with volatile exchange rates might hedge its currency risks. By locking in favorable exchange rates or pricing products in the local currency, the business can minimize financial uncertainty and protect its profit margins.

How about a business entering a region where inflation is rampant? To address the reduction in consumer purchasing power, the business could adjust its offerings to focus on smaller, more affordable options or explore bundling strategies that provide better value for money.

Lastly, let me give you a more recent example: take American businesses that were dependent on the **De Minimis Exemption rule**, which was a U.S. trade rule that allowed goods valued under USD $800 to enter the country without paying duties or taxes, with expedited clearance. The removal of this exemption led to higher production costs for businesses, effectively acting as a new tariff.

Businesses can use this as an opportunity to secure domestic production and streamline processes to mitigate reliance on foreign materials. Additionally, they could explore FTZs, or **Foreign Trade Zones**, which can delay or reduce duty payments, improve cash flow, and exempt state and local inventory taxes.

This is a very real-world, detailed example that highlights the importance of businesses being conscious of how they operate within the rules of the country in which they wish to do business. So negotiating free trade agreements may be an effective strategy initially, but it may not stand up to political pressure or cultural changes.

Wrap-Up

Global economics is the backdrop to every business decision in international markets. Exchange rates, tariffs, and free trade agreements are not just abstract concepts but tangible forces shaping the opportunities and risks of global trade.

While exchange rates require vigilance and strategy, tariffs and free trade agreements demand a nuanced understanding of their benefits and drawbacks. By staying informed, adapting to local conditions, and anticipating economic trends, business owners can navigate these complexities and position themselves for sustainable growth in the dynamic world of international markets.

Chapter 11 Practice Questions: Global Economics and International Markets

Now is the time to test your knowledge, below are a few practice questions that you can answer to gauge your understanding of the chapter. Be sure to refer back to the chapter to refresh your memory, also the answers are at the back of the book.

1. Multiple Choice
Which of the following best illustrates the impact of exchange rate fluctuations on a business?
a) A local bakery raising bread prices due to rising flour costs
b) A U.S. company selling products in Europe finds its goods more expensive because the dollar

strengthens against the euro

c) A company introducing a loyalty program to retain customers

d) A factory reducing production due to labor strikes

2. True or False

Tariffs always benefit consumers by lowering the cost of imported goods.

3. Explain

Explain how a business can strategically enter an international market while managing risks related to tariffs, exchange rates, and local economic conditions. Provide an example to support your answer.

Chapter 12: Data, Forecasting, and Market Trends

Data, Forecasting, and Market Trends are the tools businesses and policy makers use to understand what's happening now, anticipate what's coming next, and spot patterns in the marketplace. Data or economic indicators give you the facts—numbers like inflation rates, unemployment figures, or sales results.

Forecasting uses that data to make predictions, helping you plan for future demand, costs, or opportunities. Market trends reveal ongoing shifts in consumer behavior, technology, or the economy that can guide strategy. Together, these tools help business owners make informed decisions, reduce risks, and take advantage of opportunities before the competition does.

CPI (Consumer Price Index) and PCE (Personal Consumption Expenditures): Tracking the Cost of Living

The **Consumer Price Index (CPI)** measures the average change in prices that consumers pay for a basket of goods and services over time. Think of CPI as a "cost of living tracker" that reflects how prices fluctuate for everyday items like groceries, housing, and transportation.

CPI is often used to gauge inflation—when prices rise across the board, reducing purchasing power. For business owners, a rising CPI might mean higher operational costs and more price-sensitive customers. You could respond by offering discounts, emphasizing value, or finding ways to cut production costs.

However, CPI has its critics. It doesn't account for all spending categories (such as investment assets), and its methodology can distort actual inflation rates. For example, CPI measures the cost of a fixed basket of goods, which doesn't always reflect how people adjust their purchasing habits over time.

Interestingly, the **Federal Reserve**—the central bank responsible for monetary policy in the United States—prefers different inflation measures: the **Personal Consumption Expenditures (PCE) Price Index** and **Core Personal Consumption Expenditures (Core PCE) Price Index**, which excludes food and energy price fluctuations. PCE is considered more comprehensive because it accounts for changes in consumer behavior, such as substituting cheaper alternatives when prices rise. Core PCE is an even more comprehensive inflation measure because it excludes food and energy from the CPI, as these goods tends to fluctuate more dramatically in pricing than other goods.

GDP (Gross Domestic Product): The Economy's Scorecard

GDP measures the total value of all goods and services produced within a country. It's often used to assess whether an economy is growing or contracting. A healthy, growing GDP suggests strong economic activity and consumer confidence, which might encourage you to invest in expansion, new products, or hiring.

However, GDP is far from flawless. Over time, the methodology for calculating GDP has changed, incorporating adjustments for inflation, technological progress, and even illegal activities like black-market transactions (in some countries). These changes can make it difficult to compare GDP figures across decades or between countries. **Real GDP** may be a better measure of economic growth because it accounts for inflation, i.e excess government spending and taxation.

Moreover, GDP doesn't always reflect the full picture. For example, it excludes unpaid work like caregiving and overlooks income inequality. Also modern GDP numbers do not take into account government spending on social programs, immigration, or subsidies. So because of this the number itself can be overly influenced by excess government spending. A rising GDP might make the economy look strong, but reality it might not be sustainable, or give a real picture of what the economy is really like.

Unemployment Rates: The Labor Market's Pulse

Unemployment rate measure the percentage of people in the workforce who are jobless but actively seeking work. A low unemployment rate often indicates a healthy economy, with more people earning and spending. For business owners, this could mean opportunities to sell higher-end products or services.

On the flip side, high unemployment may signal economic challenges, with customers focusing on essentials rather than luxuries. In such cases, you might shift your strategy to emphasize affordability or introduce financing options.

However, the way unemployment is calculated has also changed over time. Modern unemployment rates underreport joblessness by excluding discouraged workers (those who've stopped looking for work) or people working part-time who want full-time jobs. Also it only takes into account individuals who have only been unemployed for a short time, not those who have been unemployed for a long time.

This inconsistency makes it important to pair unemployment data with other metrics, such as labor force participation rates, to get a clearer picture of economic conditions.

Labor Force Participation Rate: Beyond Unemployment

Unlike the unemployment rate, which only measures those actively seeking work, the **labor force participation rate** shows what percentage of working-age people are actually in the job market. This is crucial for understanding the true strength of the workforce.

A low participation rate may indicate discouraged workers have stopped looking for jobs, even if the unemployment rate looks low. For businesses, it can signal labor shortages or recruitment challenges. For marketers, it affects consumer purchasing power, if fewer people are working, demand may shrink. Students can see this as an example of how headline numbers (like unemployment) often don't tell the full story.

Balance of Trade: Understanding Deficits and Surpluses

The balance of trade measures the difference between a country's exports and imports. A trade surplus occurs when exports exceed imports, signaling strong foreign demand for domestic goods. A trade deficit happens when imports outweigh exports, which can increase reliance on foreign products and potentially raise costs for businesses.

For business owners, tracking trade balances can provide insights into supply chain risks, pricing pressures, and emerging market opportunities. For example, a persistent trade deficit might encourage companies to source more materials domestically or diversify suppliers, while a surplus could indicate potential growth in export-oriented markets. By including balance of trade trends alongside CPI, GDP, and unemployment data, businesses can make more informed decisions about production, pricing, and international strategy.

Interest Rates: The Cost of Borrowing and the Value of Money

Interest rates, often set or influenced by central banks like the Federal Reserve, represent the cost of borrowing money and the reward for saving it. They are a powerful lever in the economy because they affect everything from mortgages and credit card rates to business loans and investment returns.

When **interest rates are low**, borrowing becomes cheaper, encouraging consumers to spend and businesses to invest in growth. This often fuels demand, higher sales, and inflation if spending outpaces supply. On the other hand, **high interest rates** make borrowing more expensive and saving more attractive, which can slow down economic activity but also help tame inflation.

By watching interest rate trends, you can better forecast how much consumers are likely to spend, how costly it will be to finance growth, and whether economic momentum is speeding up or cooling down.

Consumer Confidence Index (CCI): The Mood of the Consumer

The **Consumer Confidence Index (CCI)** measures how optimistic or pessimistic consumers feel about the economy. It's based on surveys that ask households about their current financial situation, job prospects, and expectations for the future. High consumer confidence usually translates to increased spending, which drives economic growth, while low confidence often leads to saving instead of spending, slowing demand.

But like other indicators, CCI isn't perfect. People's emotions and perceptions can shift quickly due to political events, media narratives, or short-term shocks like gas price spikes. This means confidence may not always align with actual economic performance. Still, it offers valuable insight into consumer behavior, especially for businesses and marketers trying to forecast demand.

Producer Price Index (PPI): Inflation from the Producer's Side

The **Producer Price Index (PPI)** tracks the average change in prices that domestic producers receive for their goods and services over time. Think of it as an "upstream" inflation measure, it shows price changes at the wholesale or production level before they reach consumers. A rising PPI often signals higher costs for businesses, which may later be passed on to customers in the form of higher retail prices.

However, PPI has limitations. It focuses on producers, not end consumers, and doesn't always translate directly to final retail prices. In some industries, businesses absorb cost increases instead of passing them along, which can distort the connection between PPI and CPI. Even so, PPI remains an important leading indicator of inflationary pressure, helping businesses anticipate shifts in pricing power and costs.

Purchasing Managers' Index (PMI): A Forward-Looking Business Signal

The **Purchasing Managers' Index (PMI)** is a survey-based indicator that measures the economic health of manufacturing and service sectors. Purchasing managers are asked about new orders, production levels, employment, supplier deliveries, and inventory. Since these managers are on the front lines of supply chains, PMI is considered a leading indicator, it gives a snapshot of where the economy might be headed before other data becomes available.

A PMI above 50 indicates expansion, while a reading below 50 signals contraction. But PMI is not flawless, it relies on survey responses and sentiment, which can sometimes exaggerate trends. Still, businesses, policymakers, and investors watch PMI closely because it provides early warning signs of shifts in demand, supply chain disruptions, or broader economic slowdowns.

Stock Market Indices: Confidence, Not the Whole Economy

Indices like the **S&P 500**, **Dow Jones**, **Russell 2000**, and **Nasdaq** are often used as shorthand for the economy's health. They reflect investor confidence, corporate earnings expectations, and economic outlook. For businesses, a rising market might signal easier access to capital and a more optimistic consumer base.

However, the stock market is not the economy. It tends to reflect the performance of large, publicly traded companies and can be detached from what small businesses or average households experience. Students should see stock indices more as sentiment indicators rather than hard measures of economic strength. For marketers, the indices can foreshadow shifts in consumer optimism—or pessimism.

Making Data-Driven Business Decisions Using Economic Insights

Economic indicators are valuable, but they're most powerful when combined with your business's unique data. Let's make this practical:

Imagine you own a clothing boutique. If CPI is rising, you know inflation is making everything more expensive for your customers. You might adjust by stocking more affordable items, running promotions, or focusing on durable, high-value pieces that justify the price.

Also by looking at PCE, you might consider creating more cheaper/affordable alternatives to your original products, to capture more of the market.

Now, suppose GDP is showing steady growth. This could signal a strong economy, where customers are more willing to splurge. You might decide to introduce premium products or invest in a marketing campaign to attract higher-end customers.

But if GDP slows and unemployment rises, it's time to pivot. You might reduce inventory of luxury items, focus on staples, and double down on customer retention efforts.

Economic data can also help with timing. For example, if forecasts suggest a strong holiday season, you can ramp up advertising and inventory to meet demand. If a slowdown is expected, you can tighten budgets and focus on maintaining steady sales.

These are just scenarios, being that these metrics unfortunately can be easily manipulated and misused, you should use the multiple data scores and actual conversation from your customer base to make your final decisions.

Wrap-Up

Economic data provides a wealth of insights, but it's not a magic wand. By understanding indicators like CPI, PCE, GDP, interest rates, and unemployment rates, and recognizing their limitations, you can make smarter, more strategic decisions for your business, marketing efforts, or studies.

No single metric tells the whole story. The real power comes from combining economic indicators with your own internal data, customer feedback, and broader industry trends. This holistic approach allows you to navigate uncertainty, anticipate changes, and seize opportunities as they arise.

Ultimately, the goal isn't to predict the future perfectly. It's to respond intelligently, adapt quickly, and make decisions that position you for long-term success—no matter what the market throws your way.

Chapter 12 Practice Questions: Data, Forecasting, and Market Trends

Now is the time to test your knowledge, below are a few practice questions that you can answer to gauge your understanding of the chapter. Be sure to refer back to the chapter to refresh your memory, also the answers are at the back of the book.

1. Multiple Choice
Which economic indicator measures the average change in prices that consumers pay for a fixed basket of goods and services over time?
a) GDP
b) CPI
c) PPI
d) PMI

2. True or False
A rising Producer Price Index (PPI) always directly causes consumer prices to increase.

3. Explain
Explain how a business could use a combination of GDP, CPI, and consumer confidence data to make strategic decisions about inventory and product pricing. Provide an example to support your answer.

Chapter 13: Economic Schools of Thought: Different Lenses, Different Lessons

When it comes to understanding economics, there isn't just one way of looking at the world. Over time, different schools of thought have developed, each offering its own lens for interpreting markets, governments, and business decisions. For students, these theories provide a foundation for understanding how economies function. For businesses, they offer insights into strategy and decision-making. And for marketers, they highlight how consumer behavior, policy, and global forces can shape demand.

This chapter explores the major schools of economic thought; Classical, Keynesian, Monetarist, Austrian, and Behavioral, and shows how their lessons apply across education, business, and marketing.

Classical Economics: The Power of Free Markets

Classical economics, rooted in the work of Adam Smith and David Ricardo, argues that economies work best when left largely alone. The central belief is that individuals, pursuing their own self-interest, unintentionally create benefits for society through competition and efficiency; a concept known as the "invisible hand." Markets, if left free of government interference, are believed to naturally balance supply and demand, set fair prices, and promote growth. This perspective laid the foundation for capitalism and continues to influence debates about deregulation, taxes, and trade.

- **Students** can learn how foundational ideas about free markets and self-regulation shaped modern economics.

- **Businesses** can see the value in minimizing unnecessary costs and trusting that competition drives efficiency.

- **Marketers** can use the concept of natural demand to recognize when consumer needs will pull products forward without heavy intervention.

Keynesian Economics: Demand Drives Growth

Keynesian economics, developed by John Maynard Keynes during the Great Depression, challenged the idea that markets always self-correct in the short run. Keynes argued that during recessions, businesses and consumers often stop spending, leading to widespread unemployment and stagnation. To break the cycle, governments must step in with policies like public works programs, tax cuts, or direct spending to stimulate demand. By jump-starting economic activity, governments can restore confidence and push the economy back toward growth. This school of thought remains especially influential during times of crisis, such as the 2008 financial meltdown and the COVID-19 pandemic.

- **Students** gain insight into how governments step in during recessions.
- **Businesses** can prepare for how fiscal policies affect consumer spending and investment.
- **Marketers** can spot opportunities when increased government spending or consumer stimulus boosts buying power.

Monetarism: Controlling the Money Supply

Monetarism, championed by Milton Friedman in the mid-20th century, places central importance on the role of money in the economy. Monetarists argue that inflation—rising prices results from too much money circulating relative to goods and services. Instead of heavy government spending or intervention, they believe the key to stability lies in controlling the money supply through central banks. Tools like adjusting interest rates, regulating credit, or managing liquidity are central to this approach. This school of thought gained traction in the 1970s and 80s, particularly in response to high inflation, and still influences central banking policies today.

- **Students** can connect inflation, interest rates, and money supply to real-world financial systems.
- **Businesses** can better anticipate changes in borrowing costs and price levels.
- **Marketers** can adapt strategies when inflation reduces purchasing power or when low interest rates create more demand.

Austrian Economics: Individual Choice and Free Markets

Austrian economics, rooted in the works of Carl Menger, Ludwig von Mises, and Friedrich Hayek, emphasizes the role of individual decision-making, entrepreneurship, and spontaneous order in shaping markets. Unlike Keynesians or Monetarists, Austrians are skeptical of government intervention, believing it distorts natural market processes and hampers innovation. They argue that recessions are natural corrections to past excesses and should be allowed to run their course rather than being artificially propped up. This school highlights the importance of creativity, risk-taking, and the organic evolution of markets.

- **Students** learn the importance of human decision-making in shaping markets.
- **Businesses** can take inspiration from the entrepreneurial spirit and agility emphasized by this school.
- **Marketers** can appreciate how consumer preferences and innovation drive demand more than regulation or policy.

Wrap-Up

Each school of thought brings something valuable to the table. By studying them, students get a fuller picture of economics, businesses gain strategic tools, and marketers learn how to better connect with consumers.

To recap:

- **Classical economics** emphasizes efficiency and self-regulation.
- **Keynesian economics** highlights the importance of demand and government intervention.
- **Monetarism** focuses on money supply and inflation control.

- **Austrian economics** celebrates entrepreneurship and free choice.

Understanding these perspectives doesn't mean picking one "winner." Instead, it's about blending insights to make smarter decisions in classrooms, boardrooms, and marketing campaigns.

Chapter 13 Practice Questions: Economic Schools of Thought: Different Lenses, Different Lessons

Now is the time to test your knowledge, below are a few practice questions that you can answer to gauge your understanding of the chapter. Be sure to refer back to the chapter to refresh your memory, also the answers are at the back of the book.

1. Multiple Choice
Which economic school of thought emphasizes government intervention to stimulate demand during recessions?
a) Classical Economics
b) Keynesian Economics
c) Monetarism
d) Austrian Economics

2. True or False
Austrian Economics supports heavy government intervention during economic downturns to prevent recessions.

3. Explain
Explain how understanding different schools of economic thought can help a business make strategic decisions. Provide an example to support your answer.

Chapter 14: Budgeting and Investing: The Economics of ROI

Every person should know that managing money effectively is key to success, but understanding how to get the most bang for your buck—economically speaking—is where the magic happens. This section dives deep into budgeting and investing from an economic perspective, focusing on *Return on Investment (ROI)* and marginal analysis. We'll explore how to allocate budgets smartly and discuss tools for measuring and optimizing your economic impact. It's primarily written for business owners, but it can honestly apply to anyone! Let's get started.

What Is ROI, and Why Does It Matter?

ROI, or *Return on Investment*, is a simple but powerful concept. It measures how much profit or value you gain relative to the money you spend. Think of it like planting a garden: if you invest in seeds, water, and fertilizer, you'll want the garden to produce enough vegetables to justify the effort and cost. If your garden gives you more food than the cost of planting it, you've achieved a positive ROI.

Mathematically, ROI is calculated as:

$$ROI = \frac{Net\ Profit}{Investment\ Cost} X\ 100$$

For example, if you spend $1,000 on marketing and generate $4,000 in sales, your net profit is $3,000 ($4,000 - $1,000). The ROI would be:

$$ROI = \frac{3{,}000}{1{,}000} X\ 100 = \ 300\%$$

This means you've made three times the amount you spent. Business owners use ROI to evaluate whether their spending decisions are worthwhile.

The Role of Marginal Analysis: The Fine Line of Spending Wisely

Marginal analysis is another essential concept for smart budgeting. It helps you determine whether spending a little more will lead to enough additional benefit to make it worthwhile.

Here's a real-world example: imagine you own a bakery and have a $500 monthly budget for social media ads. After spending $500, you've gained 50 new customers. Now, you're considering spending an extra $100. Marginal analysis asks: will that additional $100 bring in enough extra customers to make it worth spending?

If that extra $100 only brings in five more customers, the return per customer might not justify the added expense. But if those five customers are big spenders or loyal customers who will keep coming back, the additional investment could pay off over time.

Marginal analysis encourages business owners to weigh costs and benefits carefully. You don't just throw money at problems—you think critically about whether each dollar spent brings meaningful returns.

How to Allocate Budgets Based on Economic Value

Allocating your budget is a balancing act. It's not just about spending on what's popular or trendy but about directing money toward activities or strategies that provide the highest ROI.

Step 1: Prioritize High-Impact Activities

Start by identifying areas of your business that consistently deliver results. For example, if email campaigns regularly bring in loyal customers, consider allocating more money there rather than experimenting with a platform that hasn't proven effective yet.

Step 2: Consider the Law of Diminishing Returns

This is an economic principle that states that at a certain point, adding more resources (money, time, effort) won't yield proportionally higher benefits. For example, doubling your budget for social media ads might not double your sales. Once you reach an optimal level of spending, returns start to level off or even decline.

Knowing when to stop increasing spending in one area allows you to redirect funds to other parts of your business that might yield higher returns.

Step 3: Experiment, but Measure Results

Experimentation is essential to growth, but it should be done cautiously. Allocate a small percentage of your budget for testing new strategies, tools, or platforms. Track the results carefully to see if they perform better than existing methods. If something works, shift more funds in that direction; if not, move on.

Tools for Measuring and Optimizing Economic Impact

Today's business world offers an abundance of tools that make ROI tracking and optimization easier. Let's discuss some categories of tools and how they can help:

Analytics Platforms

These tools track where your money is going and how much value it's creating. For example, analytics software can show which advertising campaigns bring in the most traffic, sales, or leads. This data helps you decide where to invest more and where to cut back.

Financial Dashboards

Dashboards let you visualize your spending and ROI across different areas of your business. They consolidate key data points like income, expenses, and profits, giving you a clear overview of how your business is performing.

A/B Testing Software

A/B testing involves comparing two versions of a strategy to see which performs better. For example, if you're running ads, you might test two headlines to see which gets more clicks. Over time, these small tweaks can significantly improve ROI.

Budget Allocation Models

Some tools use algorithms to help you decide where to allocate your budget for maximum impact. These tools often use historical data to predict where your money will be most effective, saving you the guesswork.

Wrap-Up

By thinking like an economist and acting like a savvy business owner, you can make smarter choices with your budget. Remember, every dollar spent is an investment in your business's future, and understanding the economics of ROI ensures those investments deliver the results you need.

To maximize ROI and optimize your economic impact:

1. Understand how ROI works and use it as a guide for spending decisions.
2. Use marginal analysis to evaluate whether additional investments are worthwhile.
3. Allocate your budget to high-impact areas while experimenting cautiously.
4. Leverage tools and technology to track performance and make data-driven decisions.

Chapter 14 Practice Questions: Budgeting and Investing: The Economics of ROI

Now is the time to test your knowledge, below are a few practice questions that you can answer to gauge your understanding of the chapter. Be sure to refer back to the chapter to refresh your memory, also the answers are at the back of the book.

1. Multiple Choice
Which of the following best illustrates marginal analysis?
a) Spending all your marketing budget on one platform regardless of results
b) Calculating whether an extra $100 in advertising will generate enough additional customers to justify the cost
c) Ignoring past results and investing randomly
d) Dividing your budget equally across all channels without review

2. True or False
The law of diminishing returns means that doubling your budget in one area will always double your returns.

3. Explain
Explain how a business can allocate its budget to maximize ROI while using marginal analysis and the law of diminishing returns. Provide a practical example.

Conclusion

As we conclude this exploration of economics through the lens of modern business, it's time to reflect on the key principles we've covered and how they can empower you to run a more strategic and resilient business. By embracing an economic mindset, you'll be better equipped to navigate challenges, seize opportunities, and create a thriving enterprise. Let's break down these takeaways in a way that's practical, relatable, and actionable for you as a business owner.

Revisiting Key Economic Principles for Success

Running a business, or making consumer decisions without a grasp of fundamental economic principles is like sailing without a compass. Throughout this book, we've covered essential topics that form the foundation of an economic mindset. Here's a quick recap:

- **Supply and Demand Dynamics**: Understanding how prices and availability affect consumer behavior and market equilibrium.
- **Price Elasticity**: Learning how sensitive your customers are to changes in pricing and how it impacts your revenue.
- **Utility** and **Consumer Choice Theory**: Understanding how consumers make decisions based on the value they perceive in a product or service.
- **Market Structures**: Differentiating between perfect competition, monopolies, oligopolies, and other market types to tailor your strategies effectively.
- **Game Theory**: Anticipating competitors' moves and making informed strategic decisions.
- **Behavioral Economics**: Leveraging insights into consumer psychology to shape your business and marketing strategies.
- **Economic Cycles**: How to describe the recurring patterns of growth and decline in an economy over time, and how to use them to predicate consumer behavior These cycles consist of four stages: expansion, peak, contraction, and trough.
- **Inflation and Cost Management**: Adapting pricing and budgeting in response to fluctuating economic conditions.

- **Opportunity Cost**: Recognizing the trade-offs of every decision you make, from investments to resource allocation.
- **Production, Costs, and Firm Decisions:** Understanding how firms determine production levels, manage costs, and make short-run versus long-run operational choices.
- **Economic Schools of Thought:** Recognizing different approaches to economic theory (classical, Keynesian, monetarist, and behavioral) to better interpret data and policy impacts.
- **Budgeting** and **Investing:** How to calculate ROI (return on Investment) and use that knowledge to guide your company.
- **Data Forecasting:** How to use metrics like CPI (consumer price index), PCE (personal consumption expenditures), GDP (gross domestic product), and Unemployment rate to predict consumption and revenue.

These principles are not all theoretical—they're tools you can use to make smarter, more confident decisions in every aspect of your business.

Building Resilience Through Economic Awareness

Every person faces challenges that test their ability to adapt and persevere. By thinking like an economist, you can respond to these challenges with greater clarity and strategy.

Take inflation as an example. When prices rise across the board, it impacts both your costs and your customers' ability to spend. An economic mindset allows you to adjust pricing, negotiate better terms with suppliers, or reframe your offerings to highlight value and affordability. For instance, during inflationary periods, offering discounts on bundled services or emphasizing long-term savings from your products can help maintain customer loyalty without compromising profitability.

Understanding market cycles is equally critical. Economic awareness lets you anticipate changes in consumer behavior, prepare for seasonal shifts, and respond proactively to market disruptions. For example, if you know your industry tends to slow down in the winter, you can use that time to plan new initiatives, streamline operations, or invest in marketing campaigns for the busier months ahead.

Economic knowledge also builds confidence in decision-making. Imagine a competitor lowering their prices. Instead of panicking, you can evaluate whether this move is sustainable for them. You might recognize that maintaining your unique value proposition, rather than engaging in a price war, is a smarter long-term strategy.

For Business Owners: Economic Insight Can Help

When you understand economic principles, you elevate yourself beyond being just a business owner—you become a strategist and visionary.

For instance, understanding consumer behavior allows you to make better decisions about how to position your products and services. Behavioral economics teaches us that people often act irrationally, influenced by emotions and biases. Loss aversion, for example, shows that customers are more motivated to avoid losing something than to gain something new. Framing an offer as "Avoid missing out on this exclusive deal!" can be far more effective than simply promoting a product's features.

An economic mindset also helps you focus on long-term growth rather than short-term wins. Instead of only chasing immediate sales, you can think about building customer lifetime value—the total revenue a customer generates over their relationship with your business. By prioritizing quality, loyalty programs, and excellent service, you create a foundation for sustained success.

Finally, economics helps you adapt to changing circumstances. Whether it's identifying opportunities in a shifting market or making tough decisions during a downturn, your ability to think strategically and analyze trends will set you apart.

Final Thoughts

Adopting an economic mindset is one of the most powerful tools in your arsenal. It empowers you to see the bigger picture, think critically about your decisions, and adapt to the ever-changing landscape of the modern economy.

This doesn't mean you need a degree in economics. Instead, it's about applying key principles in practical ways—anticipating challenges, leveraging opportunities, and making decisions rooted in logic and strategy.

As you move forward, remember that every consumer decision has an economic foundation, whether it's comparing different products and services, hiring a team (for businesses), or allocating budgets and expenses. By embracing the insights you've gained, you can position yourself as a resilient and forward-thinking leader.

So keep asking the right questions, stay curious, and approach every challenge with the confidence of someone who understands the forces shaping the market. Because with the right mindset, you're not just living at the mercy of the economy—you're becoming a valuable member of it! Take care!

Glossary

Basic Economic Concepts

Supply – The amount of a product or service that producers are willing and able to sell at different prices.

Demand – The amount of a product or service that consumers are willing and able to buy at different prices.

Market Equilibrium – The point where supply equals demand; the price at which buyers and sellers agree.

Supply Curve and Demand Curve – Graphs that show how supply and demand change at different prices. The supply curve slopes up, and the demand curve slopes down.

Price Elasticity – Measures how much the quantity demanded changes when the price changes.

Cross-Elasticity of Demand – Shows how the demand for one product changes when the price of another product changes.

Inelastic Demand – When demand barely changes even if the price goes up or down.

Cost-Benefit Analysis – A method of comparing the benefits of a decision to its costs to see if it's worth it.

Utility and Consumer Choice

Utility – The satisfaction or happiness a person gets from consuming a product or service.

Cardinal Utility – Measuring satisfaction with actual numbers (e.g., 10 units of happiness).

Ordinal Utility – Ranking satisfaction without using numbers, like "I like A more than B."

Total Utility – The overall satisfaction from consuming all units of a product.

Marginal Utility – The extra satisfaction gained from consuming one more unit of a product.

Form Utility – Satisfaction gained from the way a product is made or designed.

Place Utility – Satisfaction from having a product in a convenient location.

Time Utility – Satisfaction from having a product when you want it.

Possession Utility – Satisfaction from being able to actually own or use a product.

Information Utility – Satisfaction from having the right information about a product before buying it.

Service Utility – Satisfaction from services rather than goods (like haircuts or repairs).

Consumer Choice Theory – How people decide what to buy based on preferences, budget, and prices.

Indifference Curves – A graph showing combinations of two products that give the same level of satisfaction.

Marginal Rate of Substitution – How much of one product a consumer is willing to give up to get more of another while staying equally satisfied.

Production and Costs

Short-Run Production – Production period where some inputs (like machinery) are fixed.

Long-Run Production – Production period where all inputs can be changed.

Fixed Costs – Costs that don't change with production levels (like rent).

Variable Costs – Costs that change depending on how much you produce (like materials).

Total Cost – The sum of fixed and variable costs.

Average Cost – Total cost divided by the number of units produced.

Marginal Costs – The extra cost of producing one more unit.

Market Structures

Perfect Competition – Many sellers and buyers, all selling identical products, no single one can control the price.

Monopoly – A single seller dominates the market, controlling price and supply.

Monopolistic Competition – Many sellers with slightly different products.

Oligopoly – A few sellers dominate the market and can influence prices.

Monopsony – A market with one buyer controlling the price.

Oligopsony – A market with a few buyers controlling prices.

Duopoly – A market with only two sellers.

Natural Monopoly – A market where one seller is most efficient due to high fixed costs (like utilities).

Monopolistic Market – A market dominated by one seller, similar to a monopoly.

Contestable Market – A market where potential competition keeps prices low even if there is only one seller.

Game Theory

Game Theory – Study of strategic decision-making where one person's choice affects others.

Prisoners Dilemma – A scenario where two people might not cooperate even if it's better to do so.

Nash Equilibrium – A situation where no one can improve their outcome by changing their decision if others keep theirs the same.

Payoffs – The rewards or outcomes from a particular choice in a game.

Payoff Matrix – A table showing the outcomes for different choices in a strategic situation.

Behavioral Economics

Behavioral Economics – Study of how psychology affects economic decisions.

Consumer Psychology – How people think, feel, and decide about spending money.

Loss Aversion – People dislike losing more than they like gaining.

Anchoring – Relying too heavily on the first piece of information seen when making decisions.

Status Quo Bias – Preference for keeping things the same rather than changing.

Endowment Effect – Overvaluing things you own.

Hyperbolic Discounting – Preferring smaller, immediate rewards over larger, later rewards.

Choice Overload – Too many options can make decision-making harder.

Social Proof – People follow what others are doing.

Availability Heuristic – Judging probability based on easily remembered examples.

Framing Effect – Decisions change depending on how options are presented.

Prospect Theory – People evaluate gains and losses differently, often fearing losses more than valuing gains.

Mental Accounting – Treating money differently depending on its source or purpose.

Sunk Cost Fallacy – Continuing something just because you've already invested in it.

Default Bias – People tend to go with pre-set options.

Reciprocity – Feeling obligated to return favors.

Priming – Exposure to something influences later decisions.

Confirmation Bias – Favoring information that confirms your beliefs.

Time Inconsistency – Changing plans because immediate temptations outweigh long-term goals.

Loss Framing – Presenting something in terms of potential losses rather than gains.

Herd Behavior – Following the crowd, even if it's not rational.

Overconfidence Bias – Overestimating your own abilities or knowledge.

Decoy Effect – Introducing an inferior option to make another choice more appealing.

Economic Cycles

Economic Cycle – The natural rise and fall of economic activity over time.

Expansion – Period of economic growth.

Peak – The highest point before the economy slows down.

Contraction – Period of declining economic activity.

Trough – The lowest point before the economy starts growing again.

Recession – A significant, temporary decline in economic activity.

Depression – A severe and long-lasting economic downturn.

Stagflation – High inflation and stagnant growth happening at the same time.

Kondratiev Waves – Long-term economic cycles of growth and decline lasting 40–60 years.

Inflation and Monetary Concepts

Inflation – General rise in prices over time.

Demand-Pull Inflation – When demand exceeds supply, pushing prices up.

Cost-Push Inflation – When production costs rise, causing prices to rise.

Built-In Inflation – Inflation caused by past price increases and wage demands.

Monetary Policy – Central bank actions to control money supply and interest rates.

Fiscal Policy – Government spending and tax decisions to influence the economy.

Sneakflation – Hidden inflation that consumers notice slowly over time.

Shrinkflation – Products get smaller or less in quality while the price stays the same.

Exchange Rates – The value of one currency compared to another.

Tariffs – Taxes on imported goods.

Free Trade – Trading between countries without restrictions or tariffs.

De Minimis Exemption Rule – Small shipments that are exempt from taxes or duties.

Foreign Trade Zones – Special areas where imported goods can be handled with lower taxes or fewer regulations.

Economic Indicators

Consumer Price Index (CPI) – Measures average price changes of consumer goods.

Personal Consumption Expenditures (PCE) Price Index – Measures the prices consumers pay for goods and services.

Core Personal Consumption Expenditures (Core PCE) Price Index – PCE index excluding food and energy prices, to see underlying inflation trends.

GDP (Gross Domestic Product) – Total value of goods and services produced in a country.

Real GDP – GDP adjusted for inflation.

Unemployment Rate – Percentage of people looking for work who can't find a job.

Labor Force Participation Rate – Percentage of working-age people who are employed or actively looking for work.

Balance of Trade – Difference between a country's exports and imports.

Interest Rates – Cost of borrowing money, usually set by a central bank.

Consumer Confidence Index (CCI) – Measures how optimistic consumers are about the economy.

Producer Price Index (PPI) – Measures average change in prices received by producers.

Purchasing Managers' Index (PMI) – Indicator of business conditions in manufacturing and service sectors.

Financial Markets

S&P 500 – Stock market index tracking 500 large U.S. companies.

Dow Jones – Stock market index tracking 30 major U.S. companies.

Russell 2000 – Index tracking 2,000 small U.S. companies.

Nasdaq – Stock market index heavy in technology companies.

Economic Theories

Classical Economics – Theory that markets work best without government interference.

Keynesian Economics – Theory that government spending can stabilize the economy.

Monetarism – Theory emphasizing the role of money supply in controlling inflation.

Austrian Economics – Theory emphasizing free markets, entrepreneurship, and limited government.

Investment Concepts

Return on Investment (ROI) – Measure of profit earned compared to money invested.

Marginal Analysis – Comparing extra benefits vs extra costs to make decisions.

Practice Test

Now is the time to test your knowledge, or start preparing for your AP exam or college exam, below are a list of questions that are related to the concepts explored in the book. Much like a real exam, it doesn't cover everything, but it is meant to give you a gauge of your overall proficiency, and an answer key is available at the end of the test.

Section 1: Basic Economic Concepts

Multiple Choice

1. Supply refers to:
   A) The amount consumers want to buy
   B) The satisfaction from consuming a product
   C) The amount producers are willing to sell at different prices
   D) The cost of production

2. Demand is best described as:
   A) How much producers are willing to sell
   B) The total cost of producing goods
   C) How much consumers are willing and able to buy at different prices
   D) A government-imposed price limit

3. Market Equilibrium occurs when:
   A) Demand exceeds supply
   B) Supply exceeds demand
   C) Supply equals demand
   D) Price is set by the government

4. Price Elasticity measures:
   A) How demand changes when the price changes
   B) Total production costs
   C) The satisfaction from consuming one more unit
   D) Market equilibrium

True/False

5. Cross-Elasticity of Demand shows how demand for one product changes when the price of another product changes. True / False

6. Inelastic demand changes significantly when price changes. True / False

Short-Answer

7. Define Supply Curve.

8. Explain Cost-Benefit Analysis.

Application

9. Scenario: A new video game console is released, and the price drops, causing sales to rise sharply. Which concept explains this?

Section 2: Utility and Consumer Choice

Multiple Choice

1. Utility refers to:
   A) Production costs
   B) Satisfaction or happiness from consuming a product or service
   C) Market equilibrium price
   D) Government regulations

2. Marginal Utility is:
   A) Overall satisfaction from all units
   B) Extra satisfaction from consuming one more unit
   C) Total cost divided by output
   D) Consumer's income

3. Indifference Curves represent:
   A) Production levels over time
   B) Combinations of two products giving the same satisfaction
   C) Price changes in the market
   D) Cost of goods sold

True/False

4. Ordinal Utility measures satisfaction using numbers. True / False

5. Form Utility is satisfaction from the design or creation of a product. True / False

Short-Answer

6. Define Marginal Rate of Substitution.

7. Explain Possession Utility.

Application

8. Scenario: A shopper chooses between two brands of cereal that give the same satisfaction. Which concept shows the consumer's choice?

Section 3: Production and Costs

Multiple Choice

1. Fixed Costs are:
   A) Costs that change with production
   B) Costs that stay the same regardless of production
   C) Extra costs of producing one more unit
   D) The same as variable costs

2. Marginal Cost is:
   A) Total cost divided by output
   B) Extra cost of producing one more unit
   C) Cost of raw materials only
   D) Price consumers pay

True/False

3. Short-Run Production allows all inputs to change. True / False

4. Total Cost is the sum of fixed and variable costs. True / False

Short-Answer

5. Define Average Cost.

6. Explain Variable Costs.

Application

7. Scenario: A factory spends $1000 on rent and $500 on materials to make 100 units. What is the Average Cost per unit?

Section 4: Market Structures

Multiple Choice

1. Which market has many sellers selling identical products?
   A) Monopoly
   B) Oligopoly
   C) Perfect Competition
   D) Monopolistic Competition

2. Monopoly is:
   A) Many sellers with similar products
   B) One seller dominating the market
   C) Few sellers competing
   D) Government-regulated prices

3. Monopsony refers to:
   A) One seller dominating the market
   B) One buyer controlling the market
   C) Many buyers and sellers
   D) Government intervention

True/False

4. Oligopoly is a market dominated by many small sellers. True / False

5. Contestable markets can keep prices low even if only one seller exists. True / False

Short-Answer

6. Explain Natural Monopoly.

Application

7. Scenario: A town has only one electricity provider. Which market structure is this?

Section 5: Game Theory

Multiple Choice

1. Nash Equilibrium occurs when:
   A) One player wins and the other loses
   B) No player can improve their outcome if others keep theirs the same
   C) Everyone cooperates automatically

D) Payoffs are equal for all players

2. Payoff Matrix shows:
   A) Consumer satisfaction
   B) Outcomes for different choices in a strategic game
   C) Market prices over time
   D) Government spending

True/False

3. Game Theory studies strategic decision-making. True / False

Short-Answer

4. Define Prisoners Dilemma.

Application

5. Scenario: Two companies must decide to advertise or not. Their profits depend on the choice of the other. Which concept applies?

Section 6: Behavioral Economics

Multiple Choice

1. Loss Aversion is:
   A) People fear losses more than they value gains
   B) Ignoring previous spending
   C) Choosing the default option
   D) Following the crowd

2. Anchoring occurs when:
   A) People rely heavily on the first piece of information they see
   B) People avoid losses

C) People overvalue their possessions
D) People discount future rewards

True/False

3. Hyperbolic Discounting is preferring larger, later rewards over smaller, immediate ones. True / False

4. Social Proof means people follow the behavior of others. True / False

Short-Answer

5. Explain Endowment Effect.

Application

6. Scenario: A shopper keeps buying a brand they already own even though another brand is cheaper and similar. Which concept explains this?

Section 7: Economic Cycles & Inflation

Multiple Choice

1. Expansion in the economic cycle means:
   A) Declining economic activity
   B) Economic growth
   C) Peak prices only
   D) Recession

2. Stagflation occurs when:
   A) Prices fall rapidly
   B) Inflation is high and growth is stagnant
   C) Only supply increases

D) Only demand falls

True/False

3. Demand-Pull Inflation occurs when supply exceeds demand. True / False

4. Shrinkflation is when product size decreases but price stays the same. True / False

Short-Answer

5. Define Core PCE Price Index.

Section 8: Monetary Policy & Trade

Multiple Choice

1. Monetary Policy refers to:
   A) Government taxation
   B) Central bank actions to control money supply and interest rates
   C) Exchange rates
   D) Consumer spending habits

2. Free Trade is:
   A) Trading between countries without tariffs or restrictions
   B) Imposing taxes on imports
   C) Government-controlled market prices
   D) Limiting exports

True/False

3. Tariffs are taxes on imported goods. True / False

4. Exchange rates show the value of one country's currency compared to another. True / False

---

Section 9: Indicators & Investment

Multiple Choice

1. GDP measures:
   A) Average consumer spending
   B) Total value of goods and services produced in a country
   C) Government debt
   D) Stock market growth

2. Return on Investment (ROI) calculates:
   A) How much time is spent producing
   B) Profit earned compared to money invested
   C) Total cost per unit
   D) Consumer utility

True/False

3. Real GDP is adjusted for inflation. True / False

4. Marginal Analysis compares benefits vs costs of additional decisions. True / False

Short-Answer

5. Explain Consumer Confidence Index.

6. Define Purchasing Managers' Index (PMI).

Practice Test Answer Key

Section 1: Basic Economic Concepts

Multiple Choice

1. C
2. C
3. C
4. A

True/False

5. True
6. False

Short-Answer

7. Answers will vary. A graph showing the relationship between the price of a product and the quantity producers are willing to sell.
8. Answers will vary. Comparing expected benefits and costs to see if a decision is worthwhile.

Application

9. Price Elasticity of Demand

Section 2: Utility and Consumer Choice

Multiple Choice

1. B
2. B
3. B

True/False

4. False
5. True

Short-Answer

6. Answers will vary. How much of one product a consumer will give up for more of another while staying equally satisfied.
7. Answers will vary. Satisfaction from owning or using a product.

Application

8. Indifference Curve

Section 3: Production and Costs

Multiple Choice

1. B

2. B

True/False

3. False
4. True

Short-Answer

5. Answers will vary. Total cost divided by the number of units produced.
6. Answers will vary. Costs that change depending on production level.

Application

7. ($1000 + $500) ÷ 100 = $15 per unit

Section 4: Market Structures

Multiple Choice

1. C

2. B

3. B

True/False

4. False
5. True

Short-Answer

6. Answers will vary. One seller is most efficient due to high fixed costs.

Application

7. Natural Monopoly

Section 5: Game Theory

Multiple Choice

1. B

2. B

True/False

3. True

Short-Answer

4. Answers will vary. Two people might not cooperate even if it benefits both.

Application

5. Game Theory

Section 6: Behavioral Economics

Multiple Choice

1. A

2. A

True/False

3. False
4. True

Short-Answer

5. Answers will vary. People overvalue things they own compared to identical items they don't.

Application

6. Endowment Effect

Section 7: Economic Cycles & Inflation

Multiple Choice

1. B

2. B

True/False

3. False
4. True

Short-Answer

5. Answers will vary. PCE index excluding food and energy to see underlying inflation trends.

Section 8: Monetary Policy & Trade

Multiple Choice

1. B

2. A

True/False

3. True
4. True

Section 9: Indicators & Investment

Multiple Choice

1. B

2. B

True/False

3. True
4. True

Short-Answer

5. Answers will vary. Measures consumer optimism about the economy.
6. Answers will vary. Indicator of business conditions in manufacturing and services.

End of Chapter Questions Answer Key

Chapter 2 Answers: Understanding Supply, Demand, and Market Equilibrium

1. Correct Answer:
c) The point where supply and demand curves intersect, balancing price and quantity.
Explanation: Market equilibrium occurs where the quantity supplied equals the quantity demanded. At this point, there is neither a surplus nor a shortage, and the market is considered stable.

2. Answer:
False.
Explanation: The law of demand states the opposite: as the price of a product increases, consumers tend to buy less of it; as the price decreases, they buy more.

3. Sample Explanation:
Understanding supply and demand helps marketers predict how consumers will react to changes in price or availability. For example, if a company knows that demand for iced coffee increases in summer, it can boost supply and adjust pricing accordingly to maximize sales and avoid shortages.

Chapter 3 Answers: Price Elasticity of Demand and Consumer Behavior

1. Correct Answer:
b) A small price increase causes a significant drop in demand.
Explanation: A product with high price elasticity of demand is sensitive to price changes, meaning that even a small increase in price leads to a noticeable decrease in quantity demanded. These are often non-essential or discretionary goods, like luxury items.

2. Answer:
True.
Explanation: Cross-elasticity of demand (XED) measures how the quantity demanded of one product changes in response to a change in the price of another product. Positive XED indicates substitute goods, while negative XED indicates complementary goods.

3. Sample Explanation:
Businesses can use price elasticity to adjust pricing strategies: for elastic goods, lowering prices may increase revenue, while for inelastic goods, modest price increases can boost revenue without much loss in sales. Cross-elasticity can guide promotional strategies; for example, if two products are complements, a discount on one can increase demand for the other, such as bundling peanut butter and jelly in a promotion.

Chapter 4 Answers: Utility and Consumer Choice Theory

1. Correct Answer:
b) The additional satisfaction gained from consuming one more unit of a good.
Explanation: Marginal utility refers to the extra satisfaction or benefit a consumer gets from consuming an additional unit of a product or service. It helps explain consumer choices and demand patterns.

2. Answer:
True.
Explanation: The law of diminishing marginal utility states that as a person consumes more units of a good or service, the additional satisfaction from each extra unit tends to decrease. This principle is fundamental in understanding consumer behavior and decision-making.

3. Sample Explanation:
Businesses can use utility and consumer choice theory to predict how consumers will respond to products, prices, or promotions. For example, understanding that the marginal utility of additional slices of pizza decreases can guide portion sizes or pricing strategies. Similarly, knowing consumer preferences can help firms design product bundles or discounts that maximize perceived satisfaction and encourage purchases.

Chapter 5 Answers: Production, Costs, and Firm Decisions

1. Correct Answer:
b) The cost of producing one additional unit of a good.
Explanation: Marginal cost (MC) is the additional cost incurred by producing one more unit of a good. It is a key concept for deciding optimal production levels and pricing strategies.

2. Answer:
False.
Explanation: Economies of scale occur when increasing production leads to lower average costs per unit, not higher. Diseconomies of scale occur when larger operations increase per-unit costs due to inefficiencies.

3. Sample Explanation:
Understanding short-run versus long-run production decisions helps a business plan operations and marketing effectively. In the short run, a business can adjust labor or materials to meet immediate demand changes, such as hiring temporary staff during a holiday rush. In the long run, it can invest in capacity expansion or new technology to sustainably grow, like opening a new bakery location or upgrading ovens to improve efficiency. These decisions influence pricing, promotions, and resource allocation to maximize profitability.

Chapter 6 Answers: Perfect Competition, Monopolies, and Market Differentiation

1. **Correct Answer:**
   b) One seller dominates the market with no close substitutes.
   Explanation: A monopoly occurs when a single firm controls the market, sets prices, and faces no close substitutes, often protected by high barriers to entry.

2. **Answer:**
   False.
   Explanation: In perfect competition, products are identical, so individual firms cannot charge more than the market price. Branding has no effect on price in this market structure.

3. **Sample Explanation:**
   Understanding market structures helps businesses make informed pricing and strategic decisions. For example, a fast-food company in a monopolistic competition market can focus on branding and menu differentiation to attract customers. Conversely, a utility company in a monopoly might focus on pricing strategies, customer service, and regulatory compliance to maintain profitability. Knowing the market structure predicts competitive pressures and opportunities.

Chapter 7 Answers: Game Theory and Strategic Decision-Making

1. **Correct Answer:**
   a) Two companies lowering prices simultaneously, resulting in reduced profits for both, and neither can improve their outcome by changing their own strategy alone.
   Explanation: This scenario demonstrates a Nash Equilibrium because each player's strategy is the best response to the other's strategy. Even though the collective outcome is not optimal, neither company can improve its own payoff by changing strategy unilaterally.

2. **Answer:**
   False.
   Explanation: In the Prisoner's Dilemma, pursuing individual self-interest often leads to worse outcomes for everyone involved. Mutual cooperation would produce a better collective outcome, but fear of betrayal typically drives suboptimal decisions.

3. **Sample Explanation:**
   A business can use game theory to anticipate competitor actions by analyzing potential responses to pricing or advertising strategies. For example, if a small coffee chain plans a promotional discount, it must consider whether competitors will match the discount, launch counter-promotions, or maintain regular pricing. By predicting these responses, the business can decide whether to adjust its offer, differentiate with unique promotions, or time the campaign strategically to maximize customer gain and minimize competitive losses.

Chapter 8 Answers: Behavioral Economics and Consumer Psychology

1. **Correct Answer:**
   b) A customer hesitates to cancel a subscription after a free trial
   Explanation: Loss aversion refers to the tendency for people to feel the pain of losses more strongly than the pleasure of equivalent gains. Subscription services use free trials to create a perceived loss if the consumer cancels.

2. **Answer:**
   True

Explanation: Anchoring occurs when the first piece of information a person encounters strongly influences their decision-making, such as seeing an original price before a discount.

3. **Sample Explanation:**
   Understanding behavioral economics helps businesses design marketing strategies that align with how consumers naturally think and behave. For example, using choice architecture like pre-selecting the "recommended plan" on a subscription website nudges consumers toward the intended option. Similarly, FOMO tactics like flash sales leverage loss aversion, motivating consumers to act quickly to avoid missing out. These strategies increase engagement and conversions while respecting natural decision-making tendencies.

Chapter 9 Answers: Economic Cycles and Marketing Response

1. **Correct Answer:**
   c) Expansion
   Explanation: The expansion phase is marked by economic growth, rising GDP, increased consumer confidence, and higher business investment. Businesses typically expand operations and hire more employees during this phase.

2. **Answer:**
   False
   Explanation: Stagflation occurs when high inflation coincides with high unemployment and stagnant growth. It is a challenging economic condition because measures to address one issue often worsen the other.

3. **Sample Explanation:**
   Understanding economic cycles allows business owners to anticipate changes in demand and adjust strategies accordingly. During a contraction phase, for example, businesses might focus on cost-cutting, protecting cash flow, and offering more affordable products or promotions to retain loyal customers. This ensures survival during the downturn and positions the company for recovery in the next expansion phase.

Chapter 10 Practice Questions: Inflation, Pricing, and Cost Management

1. **Correct Answer:**
   b) When prices rise due to increased production costs.
   Explanation: Cost-push inflation happens when rising costs for labor, materials, or other inputs are passed onto consumers through higher prices.

2. **Answer:**
   False.
   Explanation: Shrinkflation occurs when the size or quantity of a product is reduced while the price stays the same, not when prices are raised dramatically.

3. **Sample Explanation:**
   A business can navigate high inflation by implementing gradual and transparent price increases, emphasizing the value of their products rather than just the price, and offering tiered options to retain price-sensitive customers. Cost management strategies like negotiating with suppliers, streamlining operations, and cutting non-essential spending help maintain profitability. For example, a bakery could slightly increase the price of bread over several months while introducing smaller, budget-friendly loaves to keep all customers engaged.

Chapter 11 Answers: Global Economics and International Markets

1. Correct Answer (Multiple Choice):
b) A U.S. company selling products in Europe finds its goods more expensive because the dollar strengthens against the euro.
Explanation: Exchange rate fluctuations affect pricing and demand for international sales, which can directly impact profitability.

2. Answer (True or False):
False.
Explanation: Tariffs increase the cost of imported goods, which can raise prices for consumers rather than lower them.

3. Sample Explanation (Explain):
A business entering an international market should evaluate local economic conditions, including inflation, currency stability, and consumer behavior. Exchange rate risk can be managed by hedging or pricing in the local currency. Tariff costs can be reduced by sourcing locally or taking advantage of trade agreements. For example, an electronics company entering a country with high tariffs on imported microchips might set up a local assembly facility to reduce import costs while remaining competitive.

Chapter 12 Answers: Data, Forecasting, and Market Trends

1. Multiple Choice
Correct Answer: b) CPI
Explanation: The Consumer Price Index (CPI) tracks changes in the cost of a fixed basket of goods and services to measure inflation and cost of living for consumers.

2. True or False
Answer: False
Explanation: While a rising PPI indicates increasing production costs, businesses may absorb these costs rather than immediately passing them on to consumers. Therefore, a rising PPI does not always directly cause consumer prices to increase.

3. Explain
Sample Explanation: A business can use GDP to gauge overall economic growth and potential consumer spending power, CPI to monitor inflation and adjust pricing, and the Consumer Confidence Index to anticipate shifts in spending behavior. For example, if GDP is growing, CPI is rising moderately, and consumer confidence is high, a clothing retailer might stock more premium items and slightly raise prices while emphasizing value to capture increased demand. Conversely, if GDP slows, CPI is high, and consumer confidence drops, the retailer might focus on affordable essentials and run promotions to maintain sales.

Chapter 13 Answers: Economic Schools of Thought: Different Lenses, Different Lessons

1. Correct Answer:
b) Keynesian Economics

Explanation: Keynesian Economics argues that during recessions, businesses and consumers may reduce spending, and governments should intervene with policies like stimulus programs, public works, or tax cuts to increase demand and restore economic growth.

2. Answer:
False
Explanation: Austrian Economics believes in minimal government intervention, seeing recessions as natural corrections. They argue that markets should self-correct rather than relying on government support.

3. Sample Explanation:
Understanding different schools of economic thought allows businesses to anticipate economic policies, consumer behavior, and market trends. For example, if a business anticipates Keynesian-style government stimulus during a recession, it might expand marketing or inventory to capture increased consumer spending. Conversely, if an economy follows Austrian principles, a business might focus on cost efficiency and innovation to survive natural market corrections.

Chapter 14 Answers: Budgeting and Investing: The Economics of ROI

1. Multiple Choice Answer:
b) Calculating whether an extra $100 in advertising will generate enough additional customers to justify the cost.
Explanation: Marginal analysis evaluates whether an additional investment will produce enough benefit to be worthwhile, helping businesses make smarter spending decisions.

2. True or False Answer:
False.
Explanation: The law of diminishing returns states that at a certain point, adding more resources (money, time, effort) yields proportionally smaller benefits, and may even decrease overall efficiency.

3. Sample Explanation:
A business can maximize ROI by allocating more budget to high-impact activities, while carefully testing additional spending using marginal analysis. For example, a bakery could increase its ad spend on email campaigns that consistently bring loyal customers but limit spending on experimental social media channels. By tracking results and reallocating funds where returns are highest, the business ensures each dollar spent contributes meaningfully to

profits. The law of diminishing returns helps identify the optimal spending level before additional investment stops providing value.

About the Author

Roggie "Raj" Clark is an entrepreneur and a 10-year marketing professional with a proven track record in e-commerce and digital business growth. Having built and managed successful online stores with thousands of sales and consulted for numerous marketing clients, Roggie has mastered the intricacies of online marketing, branding, and consumer behavior. He has also written several popular books on digital marketing, SEO (search engine optimization), and programming (HTML, CSS, and JavaScript).

As a former marketing manager at a fintech company—a role he secured through his own marketing and financial expertise—Roggie gained firsthand experience in financial strategy and wealth-building. This journey inspired him to share insights with amateur investors, helping them save money, make smarter financial decisions, and build long-term wealth. Raj currently lives in Maryland with his sister and niece.

www.ingramcontent.com/pod-product-compliance
Lightning Source LLC
LaVergne TN
LVHW082347200926
848481LV00012B/3487
* 9 7 9 8 2 9 5 5 2 4 3 4 9 *